Bruce S. Sharkin, PhD

College Students in Distress
A Resource Guide for Faculty, Staff, and Campus Community

*Pre-publication
REVIEWS,
COMMENTARIES,
EVALUATIONS . . .*

"**D**r. Bruce Sharkin's new book, *College Students in Distress*, should be required reading for all members of a college or university community and will be an especially helpful guide for new faculty and staff. From the student who bursts into tears after class to one who shares disturbing thoughts in a class assignment, anyone who works with today's college students will find the book's many vivid examples of distressed students familiar and appreciate the practical and clear suggestions for how to respond. Dr. Sharkin's writing avoids the use of psychological jargon and explains complex issues in a clear and direct style while still being respectful of the experience and knowledge of his readers.

Drawing on his many years of experience working in college counseling centers, Dr. Sharkin anticipates almost every conceivable misstep that a well-meaning faculty or staff member can make when trying to assist a troubled student, and he offers a clear rationale for why it is imperative to set boundaries with students who require professional psychological help. College campuses are filled with individuals who care deeply about students, and Dr. Sharkin provides compassionate and pragmatic advice for how noncounselors can steer students in the proper direction to obtain the help they need. Readers will appreciate how Dr. Sharkin demystifies the process of referring students for counseling and clarifies the rules about confidentiality. As a director of a counseling center I appreciate his focus on helping all members of the college or university find ways to work together to do what is best for our students."

Karen J. Forbes, PhD
Director of Counseling Services
and Student Life Research,
Lafayette College,
Easton, PA

More pre-publication
REVIEWS, COMMENTARIES, EVALUATIONS . . .

"In today's volatile college climate, the likelihood is greater than ever that any individual employed at a college or university will encounter situations involving students in psychological distress. Written for all college and university personnel, Bruce Sharkin's book is an invaluable resource for individuals working on the front lines who are most likely to first come into contact with these types of situations.

By drawing extensively upon his own experiences as a college counselor, Sharkin's primary goal is clear: to assist college and university personnel in facilitating an effective referral to the counseling center. Throughout the book he advises that when encountering a student in distress, noncounselors should not attempt to serve as a surrogate counselor but should work with students to facilitate a referral to the counseling center. This message should be quite reassuring to readers who often feel unprepared for and uncomfortable with the thought of dealing with troubled students. Overall, the book is quite practical and effective in its approach to helping readers feel more comfortable in facilitating such a referral."

Laura Hensley Choate, EdD, LPC, NCC
Associate Professor
of Counselor Education,
Louisiana State University

"Drawing from his extensive clinical experience with college students, Dr. Sharkin presents a comprehensive overview of students' mental health needs and how campus professionals can effectively address those needs. The book is written in a practical, engaging fashion that will make it accessible, useful, and interesting to a wide range of professionals on college campuses. Case examples and empirical findings are used skillfully to illustrate and supplement main points. Dr. Sharkin has provided a much-needed and indispensable resource that should occupy a place on the bookshelf, if not the desk, of every faculty member, student affairs professional, and university administrator at campuses nationwide."

Jeffrey A. Hayes, PhD
Associate Professor of Counseling
Psychology, Penn State University;
Associate Editor, *Psychotherapy Research*;
President-elect, North American Society
for Psychotherapy Research

"Dr. Sharkin's resource guide provides faculty and staff members, those who interact with students on a daily basis, a well researched, comprehensive, and perhaps most important pragmatic resource to identify and respond to students who are experiencing distress or who are distressing to faculty or staff. This book provides thoughtful suggestions to intervene when students present difficult and at times taxing dilemmas. Counseling Center staff members in particular will find this gook useful in developing and enhancing programs they provide to members of the university community."

Emil Rodolfa, PhD
Director, Counseling and Psychological
Services (CAPS),
University of California, Davis;
Former President,
State of California Board of Psychology

"Written for faculty, staff, and others in the college and university campus community, *College Students in Distress* is a landmark book that addresses the real challenges our campuses are facing today. Based on his years of experience as a university counseling center psychologist as well as a faculty member, Dr. Bruce Sharkin's book is an important resource for anyone who interacts with students on a college campus. As we know, college professionals who have any type of contact with students need to be well informed and prepared for situations that involve students in distress. What is particularly useful about this book is that Dr. Sharkin provides insights, general guidelines, specific scenarios, and practical solutions to help students access the resources they need in order to succeed in a college environment. With the intense media focus on the rising number of suicides, violence, and other disruptive behavior of students on college campuses, this book is particularly timely and meets an immediate need. Dr. Sharkin provides information to help us identify key warning signs and understand what can be done to prevent and respond to serious emotional and mental health problems among students.

The book includes an overview of the current issues in college student mental health, a discussion of both general and specific warning signs, as well as ways to address these issues. Sharkin discusses the symptoms of a variety of common problems, including anxiety, depression, suicidal behavior, deliberate self-inflicted harm, substance abuse, eating disorders, and psychotic behavior. Particularly useful is the section on ways to facilitate a referral to counseling, which provides specific examples of what can be said to intervene based on real world issues and concerns. Also highly valuable is the chapter on campus policies and procedures related to student mental health, which includes issues related to academic accommodations for students with psychological disabilities, psychological crises and emergencies, withdrawal and readmission, mandatory counseling, and limitations in campus counseling.

Sharkin closes by emphasizing the need for collaborative approaches to addressing students' complex challenges because responding effectively to students in distress requires campus-wide coordination. Sharkin writes using a tone that is refreshingly professional yet conversational making it both credible and readable for today's busy professionals needing sound, succinct information. Furthermore, the suggestions presented can be implemented across a variety of institutional types and sizes. At a time when an increasing number of students are experiencing serious psychological challenges, *College Students in Distress* will undoubtedly prove to be a highly recommended resource throughout higher education."

Yolanda Y. Harper, PhD
Assistant Vice President
of Student Development,
University of Memphis

The Haworth Press
New York • London • Oxford

College Students in Distress

A Resource Guide for Faculty, Staff, and Campus Community

THE HAWORTH PRESS
Haworth Series in Clinical Psychotherapy
Terry S. Trepper, PhD
Editor

College Students in Distress: A Resource Guide for Faculty, Staff, and Campus Community by Bruce S. Sharkin

Cultural Diversity and Suicide: Ethnic, Religious, Gender, and Sexual Orientation Perspectives by Mark M. Leach

Titles of Related Interest:

Alcoholism/Chemical Dependency and the College Student edited by Timothy M. Rivinus

Case Book of Brief Psychotherapy with College Students edited by Stewart E. Cooper, James Archer Jr., and Leighton C. Whitaker

Addressing Homophobia and Heterosexism on College Campuses edited by Elizabeth P. Cramer

Evidence-Based Psychotherapy Practice in College Mental Health edited by Stewart E. Cooper

Helping Students Adapt to Graduate School: Making the Grade by Earle Silber

College Student Suicide edited by Leighton C. Whitaker and Richard E. Slimak

Parental Concerns in College Student Mental Health by Leighton C. Whitaker

Stress in College Athletics: Causes, Consequences, Coping edited by Deborah A. Yow, James H. Humphrey, and William W. Bowden

College Students in Distress
A Resource Guide for Faculty, Staff, and Campus Community

Bruce S. Sharkin, PhD

The Haworth Press
New York • London • Oxford

For more information on this book or to order, visit
http://www.haworthpress.com/store/product.asp?sku=5228

or call 1-800-HAWORTH (800-429-6784) in the United States and Canada
or (607) 722-5857 outside the United States and Canada

or contact orders@HaworthPress.com

Published by

The Haworth Press, Inc., 10 Alice Street, Binghamton, NY 13904-1580.

PUBLISHER'S NOTE

The development, preparation, and publication of this work has been undertaken with great care. However, the Publisher, employees, editors, and agents of The Haworth Press are not responsible for any errors contained herein or for consequences that may ensue from use of materials or information contained in this work. The Haworth Press is committed to the dissemination of ideas and information according to the highest standards of intellectual freedom and the free exchange of ideas. Statements made and opinions expressed in this publication do not necessarily reflect the views of the Publisher, Directors, management, or staff of The Haworth Press, Inc., or an endorsement by them.

Identities and circumstances of individuals discussed in this book have been changed to protect confidentiality.

Cover design by Lora Wiggins.

TR: 8.1.06

Library of Congress Cataloging-in-Publication Data

Sharkin, Bruce S.
    College students in distress : a resource guide for faculty, staff, and campus community / Bruce S. Sharkin
        p. cm.
    Includes bibliographical references and index.
    ISBN-13: 978-0-7890-2524-1 (hard : alk. paper)
    ISBN-10: 0-7890-2524-8 (hard : alk. paper)
    ISBN-13: 978-0-7890-2525-8 (soft : alk. paper)
    ISBN-10: 0-7890-2525-6 (soft : alk. paper)
    1. Counseling in higher education—United States. 2. College students—Mental health—United States. 3. Stress (Psychology)—United States. I. Title
    [DNLM: 1. Counseling—United States. 2. Students—psychology—United States. 3. Stress, Psychological—United States. LB 2343 S531c 2006]

    LB2343.S49 2006
    378.1'94—dc22   2005026698

CONTENTS

Preface

During the early years of my college counseling career, I quickly discovered how crucial it was to work closely with others on campus in order to be responsive to troubled students. College counselors typically serve the most prominent role in assisting and treating troubled students, but their ability to do so is often contingent upon the ability of other staff and faculty members to identify and refer troubled students who would not otherwise go to counseling on their own. I see the process as akin to how firefighters typically respond; they cannot do much good unless others inform them of fires that need to be extinguished. Similar to firefighters, sometimes counselors can only help extinguish (or at least contain) emotional crises of distressed students that are somehow brought to their attention.

College counselors sometimes circulate handouts to staff and faculty on their campus about how to recognize student distress and make a referral to counseling. Although such efforts can be effective at their individual institutions, I started to consider the possibility of writing a general resource and referral guide that could be used by personnel at any institution of higher education. This seemed to be an especially timely pursuit given the increasing national concern about troubled college students. Thus, I set out to write a guide designed to raise awareness and responsiveness to troubled students without being limited to the characteristics or idiosyncrasies of a particular college or university. With that goal in mind, I proceeded to write what I believe is a useful resource for anyone who teaches or works with college students.

College Students in Distress
© 2006 by The Haworth Press, Inc. All rights reserved.
doi:10.1300/5228_a

ABOUT THE AUTHOR

Bruce S. Sharkin, PhD, is a staff psychologist and assistant professor in the Department of Counseling and Psychological Services at Kutztown University in Pennsylvania. He previously worked in the University Counseling Service at Lehigh University and has more than 15 years of experience in college counseling. Dr. Sharkin has published several journal articles, has been a reviewer for the *Journal of Counseling and Development* and the *Journal of Counseling Psychology,* and serves on the editorial board of the *Journal of College Counseling*.

Acknowledgments

Several individuals played either a direct or indirect role in influencing me in the writing of this book. First and foremost, I am grateful to my friend and colleague Lisa Coulter, who devoted a good portion of her time to reading and critiquing earlier drafts of each chapter. I also wish to thank Lisa Ruff and Susan Mangold for assisting me with various editing and formatting tasks. Although not directly involved in the publication of this book, I wish to acknowledge two former colleagues who have had a significant influence on my understanding of and approach to many of the issues and situations I address in the book: Ian Birky and Beth Golden at Lehigh University. I have also had the good fortune to work for two senior administrators within student affairs who are sensitive to and responsive to the mental health needs of students: John Smeaton at Lehigh University and Charles "Chick" Woodard at Kutztown University. Finally, I owe a special sense of gratitude to family members and friends who provided support and encouragement during the many long hours I spent writing, especially my father Gerald, Lisa, Luther, Will, and Emmy.

College Students in Distress
© 2006 by The Haworth Press, Inc. All rights reserved
doi:10.1300/5228_b

Chapter 1

Overview of Current Issues in College Student Mental Health

Working as a college counselor over the past fifteen years has been quite a learning experience. I have counseled hundreds of college students and encountered almost every type of problem situation imaginable. In addition to individual and small group counseling work, I have responded to many crisis calls and emergency situations, including calls from concerned parents, professors, and others on campus. I have even made some emergency dorm calls over the years. One fact that has become quite apparent to me from these experiences is that anyone who works in a college setting is likely to encounter emotionally troubled and distressed students. Unlike college counselors, noncounseling college personnel are really on the front lines in terms of spotting troubled students and enlisting assistance for them. However, dealing with distressed students can be anxiety producing for noncounseling professionals because they may be uncertain about what to do or how to respond.

Because most colleges have counseling or mental health services available on campus, it would seem that any situation involving a student in distress could easily be deferred to these services. Yet, in my years of experience, this does not always go smoothly. In some cases, concerned others try to handle matters themselves until the situation becomes too burdensome or seemingly beyond their capacity to help. Indeed, some situations can become extremely problematic and complicated. Numerous times I have been asked to intervene at a point where it seemed as if I was helping or "rescuing" the concerned person more so than the student. Even if someone is able to get a troubled student over to the campus counseling center, this does not necessarily mean that the referring person will no longer need to deal with the

College Students in Distress
© 2006 by The Haworth Press, Inc. All rights reserved.
doi:10.1300/5228_01

student. The student may not follow through with counseling after an initial appointment and may continue to behave in ways that pose concern.

It is my contention that college personnel who have any type of contact with students need to be well informed and prepared for situations that involve students in distress. This is imperative now more than ever because of accumulating evidence that suggests increasing numbers of students are experiencing serious psychological problems. Problems that might have been considered relatively rare among college students in the past such as mood and anxiety disorders are now believed to be much more common. The number of students who come to college with a history of psychological problems and mental health treatment, including psychiatric medication use, appears to be growing. Hence, the odds may be greater today for anyone who works in a college setting to encounter emotionally troubled students.

This guide is intended to help college and university personnel understand and handle situations involving students in distress. It is important to note that I do not intend to impart basic counseling skills or suggest in any way that noncounselors take on a pseudo-counseling role. Even situations that appear fairly innocuous at first (e.g., a student upset about failing a test) could potentially become much more troublesome and complex. I learned long ago in my counseling work that the severity of a student's problem is not always readily apparent in the first few counseling sessions. Thus, I believe that noncounselors should maintain clear role boundaries and avoid assuming counseling-like roles even on a limited basis. In my opinion, it can be much harder to make a referral to a professional when someone has been serving as a surrogate counselor. This book offers suggestions for responding to students primarily with the goal of referring students to counseling professionals.

Before proceeding with the task of showing how college personnel can identify and intervene with distressed college students, it is important to first discuss recent trends in college student mental health and how today's students are believed to be more prone to serious emotional and psychological difficulties. I will discuss societal changes and other factors that might account for changes in the mental health of today's college students. In addition, I address how mental health problems can have a negative impact on academic and social functioning. I also touch on the issue of how much responsibility colleges and their personnel, as opposed to parents, need to assume for the mental health care of students. Finally, I provide some background on the roles and functions of college counseling services. This material is intended to provide a context for understanding the nature and complexity of college student problems and the role of university personnel in responding to and helping emotionally troubled students.

ARE TODAY'S STUDENTS MORE EMOTIONALLY TROUBLED?

The issue of college student mental health has garnered considerable attention in recent years. There have been several articles in popular magazines such as *Time* (Kirn, 2003) and *U.S. News and World Report* (Shea, 2002) as well as prominent news outlets such as *The New York Times* (Goode, 2003) regarding concerns about the prevalence of mental health problems among today's college students. Some of this attention resulted from high-profile cases of student suicide (Sontag, 2002; Tavernise, 2003). Today's college students have been portrayed as generally afflicted with more serious mental health problems than students in the past. But is this an accurate characterization of today's students? My best answer to this question is yes, but with some reservations. Some evidence does suggest that growing numbers of college students are experiencing emotional problems of a serious nature, but much of the evidence is based on the perceptions of college counselors. In this section, I will examine some of the concerns raised about college student mental health and whether these concerns are justified.

The Contention of Increasing Severity of Student Problems

Since the 1980s, college counselors have been reporting a steady rise in the severity of presenting problems of students who seek counseling (O'Malley, Wheeler, Murphey, O'Connell, & Waldo, 1990; Stone & Archer, 1990). Many college counselors claim that they see fewer cases of students who present with traditional developmental struggles and many more cases of students who present with serious psychological problems.

This issue has received considerable attention in the counseling literature. Several years ago, I conducted my own review of the research (Sharkin, 1997) and raised concerns about the validity of the research findings. The issue still remains unresolved. Findings from two studies (Cornish, Kominars, Riva, McIntosh, & Henderson, 2000; Pledge, Lapan, Heppner, Kivlighan, & Roehlke, 1998) published after my earlier review did not provide empirical support for the purported trend of increasing severity. Findings from a recent large-scale study (Benton, Robertson, Tseng, Newton, & Benton, 2003) were believed to provide support for the trend, but I subsequently challenged that conclusion because the researchers failed to adequately assess for problem severity (Sharkin, 2004). The lack of research evidence regarding the trend of increasing problem severity may be due to inadequacies in the research (Sharkin & Coulter, 2005). The only true conclusion that we can make at this point is that there has been a *perception* among college counselors that the severity of problems has been on the rise.

Although the question of whether the mental health problems of today's students are more serious than they were a decade or two ago remains unclear, some indications do suggest that today's students might be particularly susceptible to certain forms of distress. Even the transition and adjustment to college, a common developmental struggle during the first year at college, may be becoming more stressful than ever for many students. The results of a survey conducted by the UCLA Higher Education Research Institute (as cited in Bartlett, 2002) suggest that the first year of college may take a big toll on the emotional and physical well-being of students. More than 3,600 first-year students at fifty colleges were surveyed during orientation and then again at the end of their first year. When their responses from the two different time periods were compared, some startling results emerged. First, there was a marked decline in the ratings of emotional and physical health. Second, there was a significant increase in the number of students that reported feeling depressed. Third, there was a significant increase in the number of students that reported feeling overwhelmed.

Other reports indicate that a significant number of today's students experience depression. In a survey conducted by the American College Health Association (as cited in Voelker, 2003), a high percentage of students reported feeling hopeless and depressed to the point where they could barely function. Researchers at Kansas State University (Benton et al., 2003) found that the number of students who came for counseling because of depression increased significantly between 1988 and 2001, though the specific level of depression in these cases was not reported.

There is research evidence to suggest that today's students may experience anxiety at higher levels than ever before. Twenge (2000) found that anxiety seems to be experienced more intensely among students today compared with several decades ago. Using meta-analytic techniques in which data were gathered and analyzed for college student samples between the years 1952 and 1993, Twenge determined that what would have been considered a high level of anxiety in the 1950s would be considered only "average" in the 1990s. Changes in how students experience anxiety can have important implications for overall mental health because high levels of anxiety are known to contribute to physical ailments, substance abuse, depression, and impaired cognitive functioning. This apparent rise in anxiety level was attributed largely to decreases in social connectedness and increases in environmental dangers (e.g., violent crime).

Although the psychological problems of college students today are believed to be more prevalent and serious than in years past, it is not as if students did not experience serious mental health problems in the past. Cases of diagnosable psychiatric disorders and serious emotional disturbance among students were observed many years ago (Reifler & Liptzin, 1969; Selzer, 1960). Indeed, the age of onset for many major mental disorders is during the traditional college-age years (eighteen to twenty-four); thus, a certain percentage of students have always first experienced serious mental health problems while in college. But many who work in college counseling believe that diagnosable conditions such as mood and anxiety disorders are now much more prevalent, at least among students who seek professional counseling help on campus.

Concern has also been raised about increasing numbers of students coming to college already having a history of psychological problems. College counseling center directors have reported seeing greater numbers of students with a history of treatment for mental health problems (Bishop, 2002). From my own experience, it certainly seems as if increasing numbers of students who seek counseling for the first time in college have already been in some type of treatment for serious mental health problems such as clinical depression, self-injurious and suicidal behavior, psychotic disorders, substance abuse, eating disorders, and other diagnosable disorders. The nature of prior treatment can range from brief counseling to inpatient hospitalization. Sometimes these earlier treatments date back to a student's pre-teen or early teenage years. Not surprisingly, students with preexisting mental health problems will often exhibit problematic behavior once in college, largely in response to the stress and pressures of campus life. An influx of students with such histories will place an additional burden on colleges, particularly in terms of providing counseling and other support services.

Although I have been critical of research methods used to assess for increasing severity of student mental health problems (Sharkin, 1997, 2004), I share the perception that more students seem to present in counseling for problems of a severe nature. By severe, I mean problems that cause significant disruption to a student's ability to function within the college environment and may require mental health care beyond the capacity of the average campus counseling service. I also have the impression that students today seem to be generally more afflicted with mental health problems and less equipped to cope effectively with the everyday problems of college life. There may be various reasons for why this might be so, some of which will be discussed later. It seems evident to me from my experience of observing and counseling college students over the past several years that more and more students seem to get overwhelmed by the day-to-day frustrations and disappointments of college life, be it a poor grade on a test, not getting into a fraternity or sorority, or problems in dating and relationships.

The Proliferation of Psychotropic Medication Use

There have been reports of increasing numbers of college students taking psychotropic medication (Young, 2003). Based on a sample of students seen in the counseling service at New York University over a ten-year period, Grayson, Schwartz, and Commerford (1997) provided evidence for a rise in psychotropic medication use, particularly antidepressants such as Paxil and Zoloft. Some students are started on medication before they even get to college. Indeed, more children and adolescents are being treated with psychotropic medications for mood and behavior problems (Kluger, 2003). Medications are increasingly used to help young people cope with depression, bipolar disorder, acute anxiety, panic attacks, social anxiety, and other emotional disturbances. For college students in particular, the movement toward brief treatment models in college counseling (largely due to the high demand for services) has resulted in a greater reliance on medications as a form of treatment.

Concerns have been raised about students being placed on medication too quickly and generally relying on medication to help students cope with problems of everyday life (Carter & Winseman, 2003). Today's students have grown up in a culture in which medication use for psychological troubles is common, and many have seen their parents use such medications. Some students may now see medication as a quick fix and easier alternative to counseling. Use of medication is more socially acceptable than in the past, and students may be less inclined to hide their use of medication from their peers. Indeed, use of medication may seem almost trendy in today's world.

Although medication may make it possible for more students to attend and remain in college, medication use among college students does have costs and consequences. For example, students may experience troubling side effects from medications that can interfere with academic and social functioning. In addition, college students may not properly monitor their medication use and may be vulnerable to misuse, dependency, or various forms of alcohol or substance abuse while on medication (Whitaker, 1992). Additional concerns were raised in 2004 when the Food and Drug Administration (FDA) ordered that all antidepressants carry warnings that they increase the risk of suicidal thinking and behavior in children and adolescents. This followed from a health advisory that depression and suicidal behavior could actually worsen when psychopharmacological treatment is first initiated or changes in dose are made (Stein, 2004). These concerns may be tempered somewhat by recent research findings (Simon, Savarino, Operskalski, & Wang, 2006) showing that the risk of suicide actually decreases after treatment with antidepressant medication is initiated.

Influence of Societal Changes on Student Mental Health

If indeed college students today are presenting with more serious psychological problems than students from fifteen to twenty years ago, how might we account for such changes in the mental health of students? One potential factor is the passage of the Americans with Disabilities Act (ADA, 1990). This allows more people to attend college who might otherwise not have been able to before the act was passed. The definition of disability includes mental as well as physical impairments. Hence, students diagnosed with mood disorders, anxiety disorders, personality disorders, schizophrenia, eating disorders, and pervasive developmental disorders can not only attend college but also may qualify for special assistance and reasonable accommodations. Although this has helped many more young people obtain a college education, it has also placed a tremendous burden on colleges to assist such students. Most campuses must now provide services exclusively devoted to students with mental as well as physical disabilities. The need to provide special accommodations to students with mental disabilities can affect and involve faculty, counselors, residence hall personnel, and other students.

As already noted, the use of medications for treating psychological disorders has contributed to more students with diagnosed disorders being able to attend college. Some students who qualify under the ADA may be allowed special accommodations because of the side effects of medication if they interfere with academic functioning. For example, students might be excused from having to attend class on a regular basis if their medication causes them to feel fatigued. Again, with situations such as this the burden will fall on the college to accommodate or assist students throughout their college years.

Another factor that may account for differences in students today versus the past is the enormous pressure on today's college students to achieve academic success. Some counselors believe that the pressure to succeed academically has never been higher. These days, just getting into college, particularly the more elite schools, is an extremely stressful endeavor. Once accepted, students feel pressure to excel and show that they are worthy of having been accepted. Because the cost of college has skyrocketed over the past several years, students feel intense pressure to achieve academic success to justify the financial commitment, whether through mounting student loan debt or the assistance of their parents. I have heard many students express despair over not doing well in college, especially because they felt that they were disappointing their parents who were spending a lot of money for college or because the students themselves were getting into significant debt. It is hard enough these days to deal with the increasing cost of college, but it becomes even more important to show good results for all of the money spent.

In general, there may be more financial stress on today's students. In contrast with students in the past, today's students are prone to accumulate credit card debt while still in college (Norvilitis, Szablicki, & Wilson, 2003) and then graduate with insurmountable amounts of debt only to encounter limited employment opportunities. Unemployment figures for workers ages sixteen to twenty-four have been high, around 12 percent in recent years, with college graduates facing poor employment prospects (Rawe, 2002). If such limited employment prospects continue into the future, pressure is likely to intensify for students to excel in order to compete in a limited job market.

Today's college students may also experience more pressure to succeed in domains other than academics while in college. Over the past decade or so, there has been a growing tendency for parents to involve their children in all types of activities starting at an early age. Parents may unwittingly impose pressure on their children to achieve success in multiple activities, be it athletics, music, or other extracurricular activities. By the time these children reach college age, they are already well versed in this culture of overachieving, in which self-worth and identity are derived from how much they can accomplish. The level of competitiveness intensifies at the college level, and for many, it can be devastating to be unable to perform or achieve success as one once did. I have counseled many students who experience depression and despair over no longer having the ability to excel as they used to in athletics or other areas, representing a significant loss of identity and self-esteem.

Horning (1998) believes that changes in social norms may also account for changes in mental health attitudes and experiences of today's college students. For example, she believes that the proliferation of talk shows and other television programs that address personal and sensitive issues related to mental health may have had a powerful influence on the way young people think about and discuss such issues.

Exposure to this type of repeated public airing of personal problems has perhaps resulted in more openness and willingness among young people to disclose about emotional and psychological problems, and more acceptance of treatment for mental health problems. As such, students may be more prone to reveal, intentionally or unintentionally, their emotional problems to professors and others at school. Horning describes how more students seem to be "baring their souls" in their writing composition and other assignments. Students disclose about family problems, depression, childhood abuse, self-harm, and suicidal thoughts. Students may simply be more self-absorbed and preoccupied with their personal problems.

Finally, changes in the structure of the American family are also believed by many to have had a negative effect on the mental health of young people. For instance, the fact that more children grow up in either single-parent families or in families in which both parents work full-time may result in parents being less available and providing inadequate supervision. Concerns have been raised about the diminishing quality of family life and values as well as a lessening sense of community and extended family. Such changes in the quality of family life may have created a new generation of college students who seek out surrogate parent figures at college for help and emotional support with problems that may have been neglected by parents.

IMPACT OF MENTAL HEALTH PROBLEMS ON ACADEMIC FUNCTIONING AND CAMPUS LIFE

Mental health problems can have a profound effect on several aspects of campus life (Kitzrow, 2003). In particular, there is concern about how students' mental health problems can have detrimental effects on their academic performance. Mental health problems can interfere with class attendance, concentration, memory, motivation, persistence, and study habits, to the point where functioning is significantly impaired. More poorly adjusted students, such as those who are depressed or have poor coping capabilities, are less likely to manage their study environment, persist despite difficulties or distractions, or seek academic assistance when needed (Brackney & Karabenick, 1995). Academic performance is particularly likely to be negatively affected in cases of depression (Haines, Norris, & Kashy,

1996) and substance abuse (Kessler, Foster, Saunders, & Stang, 1995; Svanum & Zody, 2001).

Sometimes students need to take a leave of absence or withdraw from school on a temporary or permanent basis due to their psychological problems. It has been estimated that as many as 5 percent of college students fail to complete their college education due to psychological disorders (Kessler et al., 1995). There seems to be more effort these days to retain and accommodate students as much as possible (especially if they qualify for accommodations under the ADA). In my counseling work, one of the activities I seem to engage in with increasing frequency is writing letters to professors to provide support for students who have had emotional or psychological difficulties that can interfere with their academics. I have sent many such letters of support for students who missed class or an exam or failed to complete an assignment on time due to emotional problems. Increasingly, instructors and administrators appear willing to take into consideration student mental health problems in terms of how they may affect academic performance.

Mental health difficulties can also be disruptive to students' interpersonal and social functioning. In addition to academic pressures, students experience considerable pressure to succeed in the social domain of campus life. This is particularly true in establishing meaningful friendships and exploring emotional and physical intimacy in relationships. Mental health problems can make this aspect of college life even more challenging and frustrating than would normally be expected. Simply stated, a college campus can be an extremely tough environment for students who experience psychological difficulties.

A case example demonstrates this best. I once counseled a female student who was bright and attractive yet suffered from social anxiety to the point where she was hypervigilant and overly sensitive to how other students might perceive or respond to her. Her anxiety sometimes seemed to border on mild paranoia and made it difficult for her to participate in many aspects of social life. She had few friends and relied almost exclusively on a boyfriend for emotional and social support. However, her boyfriend was not available to her on a consistent basis, and he often threatened to leave the relationship (seemingly because of her overdependency on him). Whenever this happened, it would precipitate an emotional crisis for her.

I see more and more students like this young woman, who have psychological problems that significantly interfere with their ability to experience satisfaction and enjoyment in campus life. Many of these students turn to professors or staff people on campus for some type of social connection or support, particularly if they do not make good connections with peers. Feelings of social isolation or disenfranchisement on a college campus can be both cause and effect for students who struggle with psychological disorders. It can be especially challenging for students who lack or have limited social skills to adapt to a new social environment such as a college campus.

A student's mental health problems can also affect other students. Troubled students often behave in ways that are disruptive on campus. I once counseled a student who would talk rather openly to her roommates about her suicidal thoughts and how she liked to cut herself as a way to cope with bad feelings. It was almost as if this had become so normal for her that she had no idea that it might be upsetting to others. Needless to say, her roommates were unnerved by it. Situations such as this are tricky because you want students to reach out to others (including their peers) if they need help, but doing so can be upsetting to other students. I have even seen situations in which one troubled student has a negative or disruptive effect on dozens of other people on campus. When dealing with student mental health problems, therefore, we must also take into consideration the effect that a student's problems can have on others.

Increasing concern about the impact of mental health problems on college campuses has even led to legislative action. The Campus Care and Counseling Act was introduced in the U.S. House of Representatives (HR 3593, 2003) and in the U.S. Senate (S 2215, 2004) to amend the Higher Education Act to include a program to support college campuses that provide mental health services to students. The bill was subsequently incorporated into the Garrett Lee Smith Memorial Act, which was approved by both the House (HR 4799, 2004) and Senate (S 2634, 2004) in September 2004 and signed into law by President Bush the following month. Funds were subsequently appropriated by Congress for 2005, authorizing competitive grants for colleges to strengthen or increase student access to mental health services, including training programs for campus personnel to respond effectively to students with mental health problems.

WHO IS RESPONSIBLE
FOR STUDENT MENTAL HEALTH?

The Case of Elizabeth Shin

Another important issue that is receiving increasing attention is the question of how much responsibility should be assumed by colleges versus parents when it comes to student mental health. This debate primarily stems from cases of litigation in the aftermath of student suicide. Following a student suicide, the student's family might hold the institution responsible, for example because of a failure to recognize or respond appropriately to warning signs (Franke, 2004). In particular, parents may claim that they should have been notified or forewarned of the student's potential risk for suicide, as in the case of Elizabeth Shin (Sontag, 2002).

Elizabeth Shin was a nineteen-year-old student at the Massachusetts Institute of Technology who committed suicide in the spring of 2000 by setting herself on fire in her dorm room. Her parents subsequently filed a $27 million wrongful death suit against the school, alleging negligence on the part of administrators, counselors, and police officers. Their primary complaint was that the school was overprotective of their daughter's confidentiality and that they should have been informed of her worsening condition just before her death.

Under the Family Educational Rights and Privacy Act (FERPA), a federal law established in 1974, colleges are prohibited from releasing educational records or personal information about students without their permission. FERPA, also known as the Buckley Amendment, was originally intended to give students the right to examine their school records, which were sometimes withheld from them by school administrators. Before FERPA, colleges tended to assume a position of "in loco parentis" or parental-like responsibility for students while on campus. In the past, parents tended to allow colleges to assume primary responsibility for their children, but in more recent years parents seem to insist on having more say and involvement in the everyday lives of their children while they are in college. This can place colleges in an awkward position of trying to foster student independence from parents while at the same time trying to avoid alienating parents. According to Johnson (2004), some colleges may unwittingly foster unclear boundaries and unhealthy dependence in students by trying to placate parents. An amendment to FERPA in 1998 giving institutions the option to notify parents when students violate alcohol and drug policies may have exacerbated this problem.

Is it legally justifiable under FERPA to notify parents when a student is deemed to be a serious suicide risk? An exception in the law allows for information to be released to others without student consent if the information is necessary to protect the health or safety of students or others. This means that it might be justifiable to notify parents in some situations but not others. In addition, campus counselors may need to disclose confidential information to others without student consent when a person poses a serious and imminent danger to himself or herself, or to someone else. As Francis (2003) observes, the issue of contacting parents can pose problems when dealing with college students. Though they may hold legal rights as adults, many students are still viewed as minors by their parents. According to Francis, the critical issue is whether the parents can be of help. In some instances, the parents may be part of the problem for the student. Thus, it is necessary to understand the family dynamics in cases of suicidal students because there could actually be a greater danger for some students if their parents are notified and/or they are sent home.

I find that in most instances parents (or other family members) can be involved without having to go against a student's wishes. Students are often quite willing to have their parents contacted for assistance and support when they are having serious emotional or psychological problems. But I have also had cases in which students were adamant about not wanting their parents involved in any way because their parents were perceived as a primary source of distress. I have had some experiences of contacting parents with a student's permission only to get a negative or unhelpful response. For example, some parents show a lack of concern or otherwise minimize or dismiss the severity of the student's problems even when it involves suicide risk. Sometimes parents actually react with anger and a sense of not wanting to be bothered.

As reported by Sontag (2002), multiple times Elizabeth Shin told friends as well as counselors that she wanted to commit suicide, and she was hospitalized after overdosing on Tylenol about a year before she killed herself. Her parents were aware of the overdose but led to believe by their daughter that it was accidental and not a suicide attempt. They were apparently not informed about the many times their daughter threatened to commit suicide. It is unclear at this point why the school's counselors or administrators did not contact her parents, but I can imagine the possibility that they tried to get her permission to involve her parents and she refused. Despite the fact that she was clearly at risk, it may have been determined that involving her parents would not help the situation.

As the Shin case evolves, it is likely to prompt changes in how both colleges and parents of college students think about and handle matters involving the mental health care of their students, especially given the prospect of increasing numbers of students with serious problems and associated issues of liability. There may be a movement toward a more shared sense of responsibility between colleges and parents. Regardless of the outcome of the case, colleges and the people who work on college campuses will always need to assume a certain degree of responsibility for attending to the mental health problems of their students. As pending litigation in the Shin case demonstrates, there is the possibility of liability for employees on a college campus who interact with students in distress (Bombardieri, 2005). Hence, this makes it so critical for those individuals who work in college settings to be able to know how to respond to and refer distressed students for professional help.

THE ROLES AND FUNCTIONS OF COLLEGE COUNSELING SERVICES

University and college counseling services have a long history of serving a vital role in the overall mission of higher education (Boyd et al., 2003; Meadows, 2000). The primary function of college counseling services continues to be the provision of direct counseling interventions for students who experience personal problems that interfere with their ability to function within the academic environment. However, counseling services support the educational mission of colleges and universities in a number of other ways. For example, college counselors provide consultation and outreach programming to students, faculty, and staff, teach in academic programs, supervise and train students in counseling programs, and conduct research on a variety of topics related to student development.

The range and scope of counseling services across the country can vary depending on factors such as the size and type of institution and the availability of resources (Dean, 2000). In general, the larger the institution, the more comprehensive the services will be. Administratively, counseling centers are usually housed within the student affairs (or student services) division of the university along with other student service units such as health services, residence life, and career services. Accreditation standards deemed essential for the provision of high-quality services in university and college counseling centers are outlined (Boyd et al., 2003; CAS, 2003; Dean, 2000). Most four-year institutions offer counseling services that are accredited by the Council for the Advancement of Standards in Higher Education (CAS, 2003). Some counseling centers also seek accreditation from the International Association of Counseling Services (IACS) (Boyd et al., 2003).

College counseling centers have a long and interesting history that would require too much space to devote to in this resource guide. Readers interested in learning more about the historical roots of counseling services on college campuses are referred to Hodges (2001) and Meadows (2000). It is important to note here, however, that over the past several decades, counseling centers have evolved in response to changes in higher education such as more diversity in the student population and changes in campus climate. College counseling is now recognized as a specialized field with practitioners who work from an intimate understanding of the context and culture of the campus community (Widseth, Webb, & John, 1997). College counselors are well-trained professionals who provide quality mental health care to students (Stone, Vespia, & Kanz, 2000). In essence, college counseling services have become increasingly important in terms of how they contribute to institutional goals, ensure the well-being of students, and assist various campus constituencies to effectively respond to the developmental and psychological needs of students.

ABOUT THIS RESOURCE GUIDE

Whereas college counselors may carry the heaviest burden in terms of dealing with distressed and emotionally troubled students, other people on campus who have contact with students will likely have moments when they observe or obtain information about a student in distress or perhaps even have direct contact with a troubled student. In my years of experience, I have consulted with individuals who work in a variety of capacities on campus regarding students they were concerned about. In addition to faculty members, many individuals on campus are highly likely to encounter troubled students, such as deans, coaches, student housing staff, physicians and nurses, teaching assistants, police officers, financial aid advisors, personnel in admissions and the registrar's office, and departmental support staff.

Troubled students may first come to the attention of many people on campus other than counselors. Some students will show signs or behave in ways that concern others on campus long before counseling center staff hear about or have a student referred to them. I am often amazed at how much others will tolerate or try to deal with before taking any steps toward professional intervention, and this was one of the reasons that inspired me to put together a resource manual for college faculty and staff. I believe that this book can serve as a helpful guide and potentially reduce the number of situations that reach crisis proportions before any intervention is initiated. Although this guide is primarily designed as a resource for faculty and staff, it may also serve as a useful resource for graduate student trainees in college counseling and student personnel programs as well as new professionals in the field of college counseling.

In the chapters that follow, I provide essential information for university personnel with respect to what to look for and how to respond to students who are troubled or distressed. In Chapter 2, I discuss general warning signs that might suggest a student is having mental health problems, while in Chapter 3, I identify indicators and symptoms of specific problems such as depression and suicidal behavior.

Chapters 4 and 5 address the process of getting a potentially troubled student to be evaluated by a campus mental health professional. In Chapter 4, I discuss how to initially intervene or respond to a student who shows signs of possible mental health disturbance. Ways to facilitate a referral to the counseling center as well as the potential roadblocks to making such a referral are addressed in Chapter 5. The practice of follow-up to a referral is also discussed in Chapter 5, with particular attention paid to the potential complications associated with confidentiality of counseling.

In Chapter 6, I examine some specific issues to consider when dealing with students in distress as well as unique challenges and considerations with specific groups of students. Chapter 7 provides an overview of common campus policies and procedures related to student mental health, such as accommodations for students with psychological disabilities, psychological emergencies, withdrawal and readmission, and the practice of mandatory counseling. I conclude the guide with some final thoughts about the need for collaborative efforts among various people in a campus setting in order to respond effectively to students in distress.

Chapter 2

General Warning Signs

Anyone who works with college students, regardless of his or her specific role on campus, needs to be prepared to respond to students in distress. Perhaps the most important skill needed is the ability to detect possible warning signs. Most often, college students will display behaviors or give cues that suggest they are experiencing emotional or psychological difficulties well before it becomes obvious or apparent. I find that college students often have a way of bringing attention to themselves, whether intentionally or unconsciously. Although there are cases in which highly distressed students manage to keep their distress concealed from others, this represents the exception rather than the rule.

Some students are quite direct and open about their problems and will not hesitate to disclose their troubles to anyone who they think will listen. Such students are often receptive to getting professional help and therefore not as difficult to deal with compared with students who do not come forward so easily. For students who are not self-initiating when it comes to seeking help, the responsibility will fall to others to notice or suspect that there may be problems and to intervene as early as possible. In some instances, parents will assume this responsibility, but more often than not it is likely to be someone on campus who has more day-to-day contact with students.

In this chapter, I describe general indicators that might suggest a student is experiencing problems of an emotional or psychological nature. I first discuss the challenges associated with trying to differentiate between normal developmental issues and more serious problems in college students. I then describe forms of behavior that should raise concern: disruptive, atypical, and unusual behavior. I also discuss how academic-related difficulties may be a symptom of mental health problems.

College Students in Distress
© 2006 by The Haworth Press, Inc. All rights reserved.
doi:10.1300/5228_02

STUDENT DISTRESS: DEVELOPMENTAL OR MORE SERIOUS IN NATURE?

Recognizing behaviors that may be indicative of serious disturbance or pathology in college students can be challenging. Many college students by nature tend to engage in behavior that could be considered aberrant by adult standards but are relatively normal or at least not deviant for college students. According to Dworkin (2005), collge culture encourages participation in risky behaviors as developmentally appropriate experimentation. Consider alcohol consumption as an example. In most situations, behaviors such as drinking to excess and losing control over how much is consumed represent signs of problem drinking. However, in the college setting, these behaviors are often encouraged and valued by other students. Distinguishing normal from problematic alcohol use in college students is difficult because drinking can serve important developmental functions in the college setting such as identity exploration and sexual experimentation (Meilman & Gaylor, 1989).

Another example is eating disorders. Because these disorders typically emerge during the late teens and early twenties, they need to be considered within a developmental framework (Attie, Brooks-Gunn, & Petersen, 1990). College-age women are particularly vulnerable to eating disorder symptoms because of developmental challenges as well as our culture's emphasis on dieting, exercise, and thinness. Thus, it can be difficult to differentiate between normal, developmentally based eating problems, such as a preoccupation with weight and restrictive eating, and more severe forms of disordered eating.

As I have discussed before (Sharkin, 1997), certain types of behavior displayed by college students may simply represent developmentally based "acting out," impulsive, or eccentric behaviors that could be misconstrued as pathological. Examples include sexual promiscuity, disciplinary problems, mood swings, and dramatic alterations in appearance such as unusual hairstyles and attire, tattooing, and body piercing. All of these behaviors could conceivably be examples of struggles to establish a sense of autonomy and identity.

Differentiating between problems primarily developmental in nature versus more serious or chronic forms of psychological disturbance is further complicated by the fact that there can be a fine line between the two. An example of this is the intentional inflicting of self-harm, a form of behavior that has received increasing attention as a problem among college students (White, Trepal-Wollenzier, & Nolan, 2002). This behavior, particularly self-cutting, appears to be becoming more prevalent among college students to the point where it is not as aberrant or unusual as it once was. I have encountered many students who engage in this behavior in an experimental sort of way to see if it helps them cope with painful feelings or negative events. Sometimes students hear about their peers engaging in this behavior and decide to try it for themselves. In most cases the student who engages in this type of behavior is not at risk for suicide because the intention is not to die. Although the behavior is still considered problematic and alarming, it may not necessarily represent a clear case of psychopathology as it once did, at least not in the college population. Instead, it may be a form of behavior that some students use to try to cope with difficult feelings such as rejection and despair commonly associated with the developmental tasks of late adolescence (autonomy, intimacy, etc.).

The primary reason I wish to highlight this dilemma in diagnosing college student problems is to discourage nonprofessionals on campus from trying to assume the role of surrogate counselor for students. I have witnessed countless situations in which faculty or staff members thought they could help a student with what appeared to be a normal or situational problem, but then subsequently discovered that the situation was much more complex or severe than first assumed. In other words, the surrogate counselor gets way in over his or her head and then tries to get the student to meet with a professional.

Sometimes students with problems more chronic or pervasive in nature will initially present with problems that appear to be developmental or situational, such as a breakup, roommate conflict, homesickness, or stress. Even professional counselors struggle with making the proper diagnosis and may not have a handle on the nature of a student's problems until after several counseling sessions. Therefore, it is my contention that anytime there is concern about a student in distress, even if the situation seems fairly innocuous, it is best to try to facilitate a referral to a counselor right from the outset. Despite one's best intentions to be available and help a distressed student, any attempts to subsequently refer a student for counseling could be made more difficult once a pseudo-counseling-type arrangement has been established. (This issue is addressed in more detail in Chapter 6.)

POTENTIAL INDICATORS
OF EMOTIONAL DISTURBANCE

Disruptive Behavior

One of the more common indicators of emotional disturbance in college students is disruptive behavior (Amada, 1992). Any behavior that interferes with academic and administrative activities or adversely affects the lives of others on campus can be considered *disruptive*. The occurrence of disruptive behavior in the college campus environment has been identified as a significant problem for administrators and campus mental health professionals (Amada, 1992, 1993; Lamb, 1992). Disruptive behavior can be in the form of inordinate or inappropriate demands for time and attention from faculty and staff or in passive behavior such as poor personal hygiene (Amada, 1992). However, the meaning of disruptive behavior is not always readily apparent. Inappropriate or irresponsible behavior is not always due to emotional or psychological problems (Lamb, 1992); therefore, disruptive behavior should be considered a *potential* sign of emotional disturbance.

Disruptive behavior observed in the classroom setting can be difficult for college instructors to address and manage. Any student behavior in the classroom that serves as a distraction for other students needs to be handled as a disciplinary matter, but it might also suggest that the student is experiencing psychological problems. As an example, imagine a student who interrupts lectures by making comments without raising a hand or first being acknowledged by the instructor. This student's behavior represents a violation of classroom conduct and rules, and the instructor would need to respond to it as such. However, if the student continues to display this behavior despite repeated attempts to correct it or if the student's comments seem irrelevant or inappropriate, then this may be an indication of an underlying psychological problem.

In contrast with the classroom setting, disruptive behavior in the residential setting can be especially troublesome because it can affect other students in a more prolonged or ongoing manner and may be more difficult to deal with administratively. As an example, a residence hall director once consulted with me about a male student who often spoke to other students in his residence about death and dying.

He also placed articles, poems, and other material dealing with death on the message board on his door. Naturally, his behavior was quite upsetting to other residents on his floor, who interpreted his comments and acts as being suicidal. When reports of this student's behavior reached the hall director's office, it was decided that someone in the counseling center should evaluate the student.

After I had an opportunity to meet with the student and make an assessment, I determined that he was not actively suicidal but seemed to like the fact that other students thought he was suicidal. In a strange way, this was the only way he knew how to elicit interest in him from other students. Although it appeared to be primarily manipulative in that sense and not a case of actual suicide risk, this was still a form of behavior that was problematic to other students and symptomatic of a disturbance in his way of relating to peers. As a result, this situation was handled as a disciplinary case which also provided an opportunity for the student to utilize counseling to learn more appropriate ways of relating with his peers. This represents an example of a case in which psychological treatment was imposed as part of disciplinary sanctions. This practice is common in the college setting (Amada, 1992) and is addressed further in Chapter 7.

Atypical or Unusual Behavior

Another potential indicator of emotional disturbance is when a student is observed behaving in an atypical manner. *Atypical behavior* is any behavior that is out of character for a particular student. The duration or persistence of the behavior is an important factor to consider. Imagine for example a student who is generally observed to be outgoing, friendly, and energetic but then begins to appear more sullen and withdrawn. This would be considered atypical behavior, yet is this a sign that the student is in some type of distress?

If a change in behavior is observed on just one occasion or for only a brief period, it may simply be a reflection of the student not feeling well or having a bad day. It could also be an indication of the student experiencing something more serious such as a significant shift in mood. The important thing is to note this change in behavior, whether brief or longer in duration, and consider it a potential warning sign. As a general rule, a noticeable change in behavior that persists beyond one to two weeks may be a sign of trouble. Certainly the lifestyle of the ·

average college student (e.g., poor eating and sleeping habits) may produce such noticeable changes in behavior, but we need to be careful not to quickly dismiss or attribute these changes to certain assumptions we may make about students. Although it is not necessarily imperative to always intervene when a change in behavior is first noted, I tend to encourage others to err on the side of caution and believe it is better to overreact rather than not respond. Therefore, I usually recommend that a student be approached as soon as is feasible or appropriate when a significant change in his or her behavior is observed.

In contrast with atypical behavior, there may be reason for even greater concern in the case of unusual behavior. *Unusual behavior* is defined here as any behavior that is deemed odd or strange for college students in general. When students display strange behavior, it could indicate serious trouble, including psychotic disorders, mood disorders, or substance abuse. It is important to note, however, that odd or unusual behavior is not always indicative of a student having such serious problems. Some cases in which a student displays odd mannerisms in verbal or nonverbal behavior are not cause for any alarm, particularly if not disruptive to other students. In addition, as discussed earlier, the college student population is one in which the range of acceptable deviation from normative behavior can be quite wide. Hence, we need to be somewhat cautious in our perceptions of what constitutes unusual behavior. The difficulty lies in trying to differentiate unusual behavior that is indicative of a serious disturbance from behavior that is eccentric in nature but not cause for concern.

To illustrate, imagine a student who can function reasonably well in his or her academics but not so well in the interpersonal and social realm. In a sense, the student's level of emotional and social functioning may be severely underdeveloped to the point where he or she is quite limited in verbal and social skills. Perhaps the student does not have the ability to pick up on social cues and may occasionally engage in socially inappropriate behavior. I suspect that anyone who works on a college campus will know some students that fit this characterization to some extent. Such students will definitely be noticed and will likely raise concern about their mental health. Do such students warrant our concern? My answer is an unequivocal maybe. Assuming a student is not psychotic or having any problems academically, the behavior may be of concern only if it causes problems for others.

Using the same fictitious student, imagine now that the student is a male who inappropriately ogles female students without an awareness of how it causes discomfort for others on campus. This could be considered a form of disruptive behavior and simply treated in a disciplinary manner. Even though we are dealing with a student who may lack the capacity to behave in a socially appropriate manner, the behavior poses a problem for others and needs to be addressed as such. This could also be used as an opportunity to refer (or even mandate) the student for counseling, if deemed appropriate.

Now imagine that this same student sometimes mumbles to himself while walking on campus. He does not bother or disturb any other students but is perceived as odd or weird. Should we be concerned about this student? Not necessarily, unless some additional evidence suggests that the student is seriously disturbed. We may just be dealing with a student whose behavior is somewhat eccentric but not having a negative impact on others. I have encountered students like this in various locations on campus outside of my counseling office. In some cases, these students do voluntarily come or get referred to the counseling office, whereas others never do. In general, it is important to take note of any students who are observed behaving in unusual ways; at the very least, this may warrant a consultation with the counseling office to see if any specific action needs to be taken.

Academic-Related Problems

As discussed in Chapter 1, mental health problems can have a negative impact on academic functioning. This goes beyond just academic performance and may involve multiple dimensions of academic-related behavior. As a counselor, I often find myself helping students cope with academic struggles that result from their emotional or psychological troubles. Emotional problems can be disruptive in many ways, for instance, by contributing to poor study habits and diminished motivation for school. Although some students manage to avoid any significant decline in their academic performance even while dealing with emotional distress, students in distress generally tend to have some disruption in their academics. When emotional distress negatively affects academic performance, this can create a negative cycle; that is, distress results in problems in academics that in turn result in even more distress. A student's level of distress regarding his or her compromised performance will vary depending on the degree of investment in succeeding academically.

Aside from poor performance, the more common indicators of underlying distress are excessive unexplained absences from class and failure to complete assignments. Other indicators are based on observations of in-class behavior such as frequently arriving late or leaving early, falling asleep in class, inattentiveness, and frequent requests for clarification or special consideration. It should be noted that increasing numbers of students are identified or formally diagnosed with attention-deficit disorder or learning disabilities, which might contribute to some of these difficulties. If the condition has already been diagnosed, then it is the student's responsibility to make sure that his or her professors are aware, particularly if any accommodations are requested. If a student has not been identified as such, it is possible that some of the behaviors mentioned could be indicative of learning-related problems as opposed to emotional distress. In either case, these behaviors can be quite diagnostic and may warrant some type of intervention.

A case example will illustrate how a student's absence from class can be an indication of serious troubles. I once met with a first-year transfer student who presented in crisis because she had not been attending any of her classes and was fearful of failing out of college. This was about four weeks into the spring semester. She had transferred from another college after doing poorly in the one semester she completed there. This student seemed very bright and insightful and had done well academically when she was in high school, so it was somewhat of a mystery as to why she would have problems in her academics. It became increasingly clear that she was experiencing severe anxiety and tremendous fear about the prospect of having a panic attack in class. This anticipatory anxiety inhibited her from attending any classes. Her circumstances were made worse by virtue of transferring in midyear and not being able to obtain either on-campus housing or nearby off-campus housing. Consequently, she ended up having to live alone in an apartment a significant distance from the campus. Being a new student to the school left her without anyone to accompany her to campus and made her feel socially isolated. Her anxiety was intensified by her experience of having done poorly at the other college, which she attributed to lack of effort. Her decision to transfer to her present school had been her way of trying to start over and rededicating herself to academics.

Although I assessed her to have a diagnosable anxiety disorder that made it extremely difficult for her to attend classes, it was hard to intervene on her behalf given how much class time she had already missed. I consulted with her professors, but most of them felt that she would have too much work to make up. Thus, it was mutually agreed that she should withdraw from school and take a leave of absence for the remainder of the semester. This would give her some time to get treatment for her anxiety and better prepare her for college. Perhaps the hardest part for her was informing her parents, because she was worried about disappointing them once again.

Professors and other college personnel need to keep in mind that academic-related problems are often a symptom of emotional disturbance that may require some type of nonacademic intervention. Even academic dishonesty in the form of cheating on an exam or plagiarism can be a symptom of emotional disturbance. Cases of dishonesty will always need to be treated as a form of student misconduct with appropriate consequences, but sometimes students engage in these behaviors due to emotional or psychological factors.

As an example, a professor contacted me about a student who had plagiarized on a paper. The professor thought that this was quite out of character for the student (i.e., atypical behavior) given his previous academic work. The professor knew that she had to impose some type of punishment (and gave him a failing grade for the paper) but at the same time was willing to take into account the fact that the student seemed to be struggling with personal problems. After I had an opportunity to meet with the student, my assessment was that he engaged in the dishonest behavior largely because he was depressed. He was afraid to ask his professor for an extension because he did not want to tarnish his image as an excellent student. The professor allowed him to do another paper as long as he was willing to utilize counseling.

Some skepticism has always existed in the college setting regarding the impact of emotional distress on academics. A long history of suspicion persists, especially among college faculty, that students will make every excuse imaginable in order to avoid, postpone, or be relieved of certain responsibilities. Still, there recently seems to have been somewhat of a shift in the perspective of many professors and others on campus to more empathy and understanding for students having troubles in their academics due to mental-health-related issues. I currently serve on a committee that evaluates student petitions regarding grade changes, backdated withdrawals, and other changes in their academic transcripts. For the most part, faculty and staff members are willing to consider how personal problems can interfere with or impair academic functioning.

SUMMARY

It can be challenging to differentiate between student distress that is of a developmental nature and distress that is more indicative of serious disturbance. This is made especially difficult because of the greater degree of tolerance for certain types of behavior (e.g., heavy alcohol consumption) within the college setting that would be considered pathological outside the context of college student life. Potential warning signs can indicate that a student may be experiencing some type of emotional or psychological distress. Disruptive, atypical, and unusual behaviors are common signs to pay attention to. In addition, academic-related problems such as poor performance and poor attendance are potential indicators of underlying student distress.

Chapter 3

Recognizing Specific Problems

In Chapter 2, I addressed general warning signs to look for that might indicate that a student is experiencing emotional or psychological distress. In this chapter, I discuss some of the signs and symptoms of specific problems common among college students. Based on my experience consulting with others on campus regarding their concerns about students, I have chosen seven problem categories that seem to occur with the most frequency:

1. anxiety
2. depression
3. suicidal behavior
4. deliberate self-inflicted harm
5. substance abuse
6. eating disorders
7. psychotic behavior

Any evidence to suggest that a student is experiencing one or more of these problems is justification for concern and intervention, with suicidal and psychotic behavior requiring the most immediate response.

Although I discuss these as separate categories, it is important to keep in mind that these problems are often interrelated or may have similar features. Indeed, some of these problem categories can be manifestations of one another (e.g., depression often leads to suicidal behavior) and students frequently experience some combination of these problems. I purposely chose to exclude personality disorders from this discussion, even though they represent another serious form of disturbance observed in college students. These disorders are complex and difficult to diagnose and would require considerable discus-

College Students in Distress
© 2006 by The Haworth Press, Inc. All rights reserved.
doi:10.1300/5228_03

sion to adequately describe for people outside of the mental health profession. For the purposes of this chapter, the reader simply needs to be aware that sometimes the problems or distress of students can involve more complexity than meets the eye. As I will demonstrate, it can be important for college personnel to be able to recognize certain forms of student distress such as anxiety and depression, but ultimately it is the campus mental health professional's responsibility to diagnose student problems.

When trying to determine the nature of a student's distress, we have three potential sources of information: what the student tells us, what others tell us about the student, and our observations of the student. All three sources of information can be valuable in determining what type of distress or problem a student is experiencing, but each can have certain limitations. For example, students may be vague in describing their distress because they do not have a clear sense of what is troubling them. Even when we get information directly from a student, it may still leave us in doubt as to what the student is experiencing. Information about a student's distress obtained from others, such as fellow students, can often be unreliable because of biases, distortions, exaggerations, and misperceptions. Our observations of the student's verbal and nonverbal behavior are sometimes the most important source of information, but these too are vulnerable to inaccuracies and misperceptions.

Ideally, we would have at least two sources of information for corroborating evidence, but this will not always be possible. More typically, we will end up relying on one source or another, and depending on the type of problem suspected, some sources of information can be more reliable than others. For concerns about suicidal risk, for instance, we need to rely primarily on the student's admission or denial of suicidal intent. With eating disorders and substance abuse, we may need to rely more on what others report, because the student may deny or lack awareness of the problem. Our direct observations of student behavior may be the most reliable source of information when dealing with psychotic behavior.

ANXIETY

Anxiety has been identified as a significant problem among college students (Amada and Grayson, 1989; Benton et al., 2003). Many different forms of anxiety may be observed in college students, ranging in intensity from mild to severe, with the more severe cases causing significant problems in academic and social functioning.

Panic Attacks

A likely scenario of needing to respond to a student in distress due to anxiety is a student having a panic attack. This can occur in any situation or context on campus, particularly during social or performance situations. Some students get so overwhelmed and stressed because of academic pressures or personal problems that they make themselves more vulnerable to a panic attack. A student having a panic attack will think that he or she is "losing it," "going crazy," or experiencing some type of life-threatening condition. The use of or withdrawal from certain substances such as caffeine or sedatives as well as certain medical conditions such as hypoglycemia can mimic symptoms of panic, but a true panic attack is not due to these other conditions.

Students who are already aware of their vulnerability to anxiety attacks and have consulted with a mental health professional are likely to be equipped in ways to manage or prevent attacks from occurring. The most likely crisis scenario would involve a student having an attack for the first time or a subsequent attack without knowing that it is a panic attack. A student having a panic attack might be observed leaving abruptly from a class or meeting without indicating why there is a need to leave. Although some of the symptoms experienced during a panic episode will not be visible to an observer (e.g., heart palpitations, abdominal distress), there can be overt signs such as tremors, sweating, and hyperventilating. Generally speaking, a student having a panic attack will typically appear just as we might expect: highly anxious, confused, jittery, pale, and frightened. The student may speak in a rapid or pressured manner and appear distracted or inattentive.

Social Anxiety

A form of anxiety that can ultimately produce panic attacks is social anxiety. This type of anxiety, which seems to be fairly prevalent among college students, is characterized by a strong and irrational fear of social situations. The socially anxious student will be afraid or worried about being embarrassed or negatively judged by others, particularly peers. Some students may become so hypervigilant or hypersensitive to the perceptions and reactions of others that their distress assumes a state of near paranoia. These students are likely to avoid any participation in classroom activities and discussion and may appear excessively anxious when called upon or asked to participate.

Cases of social anxiety can emerge in response to a performance situation such as speaking in front of a class. For some students, the fear of being called on or asked to speak in class can be overwhelming, sometimes to the point where the student will skip class or otherwise try to avoid it rather than risk any anticipated humiliation. I have dealt with many cases of students who become extremely anxious about having to give an oral presentation for a required speech or public speaking course. Hence, the distress of socially anxious students may come to our attention only because of problems associated with their avoidance of certain situations, particularly performance-related activities such as a class presentation. It is important for faculty and staff members to be sensitive to the possibility that a student is having problems in the academic environment due this type of anxiety.

Posttraumatic Stress

Another type of anxiety important for college personnel to be aware of is posttraumatic stress (PTS). This condition tends to be associated with combat veterans, but I have seen numerous cases of college students who display symptoms of PTS following an assault (sexual or nonsexual) or other victimization experience. Although the symptoms can vary somewhat depending on the type of trauma, symptoms commonly observed in individuals with PTS include a re-experiencing of the traumatic event through recurrent images, thoughts, dreams, or flashbacks, and a tendency to avoid activities, places, or people associated with the trauma. Some of the symptoms of PTS might give the appearance that the person is depressed: social detachment, loss of interest in activities, irritability, sleep-related difficulties, and diminished concentration. The person might also seem hypervigilant and nervous around other people.

I once counseled a female student who was abducted from the campus by a male stranger but managed to escape unharmed physically. This experience was clearly traumatic and continued to haunt her for quite some time and made it difficult for her to truly feel safe again while on campus. I also counseled a male student who was shot in the leg following an altercation with someone at an off-campus party. Although he recovered from the physical wound, he could not stop thinking about and reexperiencing the incident in his mind and he felt much more insecure than ever before.

These two examples may seem extreme, but I have encountered increasing numbers of situations in which students are victims of a traumatic injury or event while in college that significantly disrupts their everyday functioning. Regardless of whether the traumatic event occurs while the student is at or away from school, the effects are likely to have a negative impact on the student's college life. Many kinds of situations could result in PTS symptoms. Students can be traumatized by the death of a friend or family member, particularly if it is the result of murder or suicide. I saw several students who displayed symptoms of PTS following the terrorist attacks of September 11, 2001, even in cases in which they did not have any direct connection to the attacks or the victims of the attacks.

Faculty and staff members may encounter students who disclose that they experienced a traumatic event, perhaps because they need to miss time from school because of it. In any case, PTS is another type of distress to be vigilant to in situations when it is known or becomes known that a student has had a traumatic experience.

Test Anxiety

One other specific form of anxiety that should be mentioned is test anxiety. Naturally, test anxiety is a common problem in the academic setting. The majority of cases of test anxiety are not too disruptive for students, but certain cases can be more severe. Students with severe test anxiety are likely to come to the attention of faculty or staff members. In some instances, students who struggle with severe test anxiety may actually have learning-related difficulties or other problems that generate intense anxiety about performance on exams. Therefore, when students claim that test anxiety results in poor performance or not being able to sit for an exam, further evaluation and determination of the sources of this anxiety need to be made. This typically will involve counseling or disability services, or both.

DEPRESSION

Depression has been identified as a problem for a significant proportion of students (Benton et al., 2003; Furr, Westefeld, McConnell, & Jenkins, 2001; Westefeld & Furr, 1987) and can be a major factor in why students withdraw from college (Meilman, Manley, Gaylor, & Turco, 1992). Researchers have found that college-age females appear to be more vulnerable to depression than college-age males (Nolan-Hoeksema & Girgus, 1994), though specific research with college student samples has not always found gender differences in depression (e.g., Gladstone & Koenig, 1994). In fact, some researchers have found male rather than female college students to be more predisposed to depression (e.g., Grant et al., 2002). Whether gender differences exist in the rate of depression among college students may be complicated by the potential for depression to manifest differently as a function of gender. For example, I have observed anger and irritability as symptoms of depression much more often in male than female students.

Depression is a disturbance in mood that can range in degree from mild to severe, characterized by varying degrees of emotional and behavioral symptoms. In some ways, it is not surprising to know that many students experience depression given the ups and downs of the transition into adulthood associated with the traditional college years. However, concern has been growing about increasing numbers of students experiencing more troublesome forms of depression that interfere with their ability to function in the college environment.

Several common indicators or symptoms associated with depression may be observed in students. Some visible signs are self-neglect of appearance and hygiene, significant weight loss or gain, appearing fatigued, inattentiveness (due to diminished ability to concentrate), restlessness, irritability, and lack of emotional responsiveness or being overly emotional (e.g., frequent crying). Other possible indicators that may be observed are social withdrawal, diminished interest in previously enjoyed activities, neglect of responsibilities, impaired memory, indecisiveness, loss of appetite or compulsive eating, and preoccupation with physical health symptoms that do not respond to medical treatment. Academic-related behavior that could indicate depression includes missing classes, coming to classes late or unprepared, and a significant drop in performance and grades.

Some of the more common symptoms of depression can be determined only from talking with the individual because they have to do with feelings, attitudes, or perceptions. A depressed student might express feelings of sadness, hopelessness, disappointment, loneliness, self-doubt, guilt, shame, self-blame, pessimism, worthlessness or inadequacy, general unhappiness or dissatisfaction, and being overwhelmed. Reports of increased use of alcohol or drugs (including prescribed and over-the-counter medications) and sleep-related difficulties are also possible indications of depression. Generally speaking, the more of these symptoms that are observed, the greater is the likelihood of depression or disturbance in mood. Also, the more intensely and longer the symptoms persist, the more likely it is that the student is experiencing a serious form of depression.

Some students may actually experience a chronic form of depression, with a long history of (treated or untreated) depression that they have somehow managed to live with. One critical way to differentiate normal depression from a more chronic or complicated form is whether a student has symptoms of depression in response to a specific event. We would expect a student to be depressed following a negative life event such as a relationship loss, but some students experience depression without being able to pinpoint any specific or triggering event. It should be noted, however, that even when in it is in response to a specific event, the degree of depression could become quite severe. I often see this happen following the breakup of a romantic relationship. Although such breakups can be difficult at any point in life, they can assume an exaggerated magnitude for college students, perhaps because of the importance of establishing intimacy as a developmental task of the traditional college-age years.

Another important point is that some students are able to effectively hide from everyone the fact that they struggle with depression. In effect, they put up a front and give the appearance of being happy when they are really experiencing a sense of inner turmoil. The need to mask feelings of depression can occur for various reasons, but typically there is a fear of what might happen if the true feelings were revealed (e.g., being rejected). Also, many students have a strong need to maintain a certain image or become quite invested in being perceived as always happy. I have seen this countless times in my work as a college counselor. These students will often end up seeking counseling because of the stress of continually having to hide how they really feel. It is an interesting experience to be the only one who really knows how a student truly feels, particularly with students that are perceived as happy, outgoing, and popular. Being a counselor enables me to know some students better than even their family members or closest friends.

This is something for college personnel to be aware of because there may be instances in which students such as this will feel comfortable enough to risk revealing themselves with certain faculty or staff members. This is when it might be particularly tempting to assume the role of a surrogate counselor with a student who by all accounts seems well adjusted. One can suddenly be faced with a distressed student who had always appeared to be happy and generally well functioning. I remind the reader of my earlier caution not to fall into this potential trap. As I learned long ago, things are not always as they appear.

Mania

Some students may show indications or describe symptoms suggesting problems with mood fluctuations as opposed to depression per se. Students who experience mood swings may have concerns about being "bipolar," a term that tends to be used rather casually these days without being well understood. In contrast with depression, bipolar or manic-depressive mood disorders are more complex and difficult even for professional clinicians to diagnose (Rivas-Vazquez, Johnson, Rey, Blais, & Rivas-Vazquez, 2002). Perhaps the most commonly observed behavior in distressed students suggestive of bipolar disorder is mania. Symptoms of mania include inappropriate elation or irritability, grandiose thoughts or ideas (e.g., believing oneself to have special knowledge or abilities), inflated sense of self (e.g., being overconfident and boastful), disconnected or racing thoughts, extreme bursts of energy, distractibility, and being more talkative than usual or appearing pressured to keep talking. A student having a manic or hypomanic episode might also display inappropriate social behavior and engage in behavior that may have negative consequences (e.g., being overly sexual, impulsive spending, etc.). There may also be signs of severe insomnia or a decreased need for sleep.

SUICIDAL BEHAVIOR

Mood disturbances often result in another major problem, suicidal behavior. Concerns about suicide risk generate considerable anxiety for those who work on a college campus. Anxieties have likely risen in the wake of five student suicides at New York University (NYU) that occurred over a thirteen-month period starting in the fall semester of 2003. High-profile cases such as these garner much media attention (e.g., Shea, 2002; Sontag, 2002) and can be sensationalized and blown out of proportion by the media (Kennedy, 2004). Even at larger universities such as NYU, completed suicides place increasing scrutiny on campus suicide-prevention efforts. The Jed Foundation was established to assist colleges around the country in order to provide suicide-prevention resources, including a Web site that links students to mental health resources. The foundation was named after a student (Jed Satow) who committed suicide while attending the University of Arizona in 1998.

Data on Student Suicide

Before discussing the warning signs and risk factors, it may be helpful to first present some of the data that are available on college student suicide. Although the data have been characterized as inconsistent and inconclusive (Haas, Hendin, & Mann, 2003), compelling evidence shows that the suicide rate for college students is actually lower than for nonstudents (Schwartz & Whitaker, 1990). This was a key finding of the Big Ten Study (Silverman, Meyer, Sloane, Raffel, & Pratt, 1997), one of the most comprehensive and large-scale studies (involving nearly 350,000 students) on the incidence of suicide in undergraduate and graduate students. In this study, the researchers examined data for all known completed suicides (261) among undergraduate and graduate students from September 1, 1980, to August 31, 1990, on the main campuses of the twelve midwestern schools affiliated with the Big Ten University Athletic Association. It was found that the average suicide rate across all of these campuses for the ten-year period was 7.5 per 100,000 students, which was half the rate of 15 per 100,000 computed for a national sample of nonstudents matched on age, gender, and race. The researchers suggested that the lower rate for college students might be due to mental health services being readily available on campuses compared with what is available for nonstudents. Another key finding was that the suicide rate for students age twenty-five and over was significantly higher than that for younger students.

From a statistical viewpoint, our concerns about student suicide risk may seem somewhat unwarranted. Indeed, only about 1 to 2 percent of students who contemplate suicide actually commit suicide (Schwartz & Whitaker, 1990). Even if we assume that what happened at NYU is an anomaly and that suicide among college students remains a relatively rare occurrence for the most part, we must not underestimate the devastation and potential trauma to a campus following a suicide. Even suicide threats and unsuccessful attempts can be traumatic to people on campus, especially friends and others associated with the suicidal person. I have seen firsthand how a student who threatens or attempts suicide can negatively affect fellow students. I have also had experience helping others cope in the aftermath of a completed suicide, and I can honestly say that it is one of the more difficult interventions to have to make.

In terms of warning signs, it is generally believed that the majority of those who attempt or commit suicide will give some type of clues. In my experience, college students who are at risk for suicide do tend to come to someone's attention, be it other students, instructors, or campus staff members. Students might make explicit comments ("I'm thinking about taking a razor and slitting my wrists") or ones that give reason to suspect suicidal inclinations ("Life is getting to be too much for me"). Students have sometimes used written assignments or e-mail messages to convey their suicidal thoughts and feelings. Unless they are very impulsive, suicidal students will likely be pondering thoughts of suicide well before they actually make an attempt. Although there are cases in which we will have little reason to suspect that a student might be at risk for suicide no matter how vigilant we might be, we should be able to pick up on indications of risk in a large percentage of cases. In assessing the degree of risk, it can be helpful to differentiate between suicidal ideation, threats, and gestures.

Suicidal Ideation

Whereas we may take some comfort in the fact that completed suicides remain relatively infrequent, the occurrence of suicidal ideation seems to be fairly prevalent among college students (Benton et al., 2003; Brener, Hassan, & Barrios, 1999; Furr et al., 2001; Rudd, 1989; Westefeld & Furr, 1987). Depression, hopelessness, and loneliness have been identified as strong risk factors for suicidal ideation in college students (Weber, Metha, & Nelsen, 1997). Like anxiety and depression, suicidal ideation can vary in intensity. At least from my vantage point, many students admit to having mild suicidal thoughts at one time or another without ever acting on the thoughts. They may have fleeting thoughts that stem from momentary depression or despair about things not going well or following negative events. With some students the degree of ideation may be somewhat more intense but still not mean the student is at risk for suicide. For example, in response to questions about suicidal ideation, I often hear students say that they feel bad enough that they would not mind if something happened *to* them but they would not do anything to harm themselves. This has been referred to as "passive" suicidal ideation because there is no active plan or intent to do self-harm, though this can raise concern about a student's risk for harm due to carelessness or lack of safety consciousness.

Suicidal Threat or Gesture

The level of risk increases significantly when a student makes a suicide threat, that is, when a student says or does something to indicate suicidal intent. Suicidal threats tend to be made more frequently by females than males (Foreman, 1990). Even when students make such threats, however, it does not mean that they are intent on committing suicide. There are instances when suicide threats are made to get attention or manipulate others (recall the example of the student from Chapter 2). Despite the fact that this is often the case, all threats must be taken seriously. In general, anyone who makes a suicide threat needs to be evaluated to determine the degree of risk.

The greatest degree of risk for suicide is when a student gives indication of serious intent to suicide. This includes when a student has

1. a specific plan, including the method, time, and place,
2. the means available,
3. chosen a lethal method (e.g., using a gun), and
4. made final plans or arrangements (with no reference to future events).

Making a clear reference to suicide in writing or actually writing a suicide note is another high-risk indicator. Nowadays, students will sometimes convey suicidal intentions using computerized correspondence such as e-mail and instant messengers. In general, the more specific a student is about his or her intent to commit suicide, the more need there is for an immediate response or intervention.

Interestingly, one study found that the majority of students who made suicide threats were in counseling at the time they made the threat (Meilman, Pattis, & Kraus-Zeilmann, 1994). This is a sobering reminder that being in counseling does not necessarily result in diminished suicidal thoughts or threats. In addition, students may conceal or minimize their suicidal thoughts and tendencies from their counselor in some situations; therefore, even if a student is in counseling already, it should never be assumed that the student could not be at risk for suicide.

A student may make what is characterized as a suicidal gesture, which is typically considered a self-destructive act of low lethality and thus not likely to result in death. Women may be more prone than men to suicidal gestures (Foreman, 1990). Such gestures do not always result in a need for medical attention and thus may not become known to others. Though a gesture may be viewed as a proverbial "cry for help," it clearly increases the student's risk for a subsequent attempt. Sometimes students who are not really intent on dying do something that unwittingly results in serious injury; thus, we should not necessarily be any less concerned about the prospect of a gesture as opposed to an attempt.

Additional Risk Factors

It is important to be aware of additional risk factors, some based on demographics, which have been identified through research on suicide. Those students found to be most at risk for committing suicide are males, substance abusers, students who are socially isolated, depressed, psychotic or schizophrenic, and international students (Schwartz & Whitaker, 1990). Asian-American females have been identified as a specific college population that may be particularly vulnerable to episodes of suicidal ideation and attempts (Chung, 2003). Characteristics and traits that have been associated with suicide risk are poor impulse control, anger and hostility, and preoccupation with thoughts about death and dying. In their study of students who attempted suicide, Meilman et al. (1994) found that over 90 percent of the attempters had experienced a recent failure in work and school and many had experienced problems in a romantic relationship. Recent losses, including relationships, resources, or abilities, as well as poor academic performance, have been associated with increased risk. The more risk factors that apply, the greater the degree of risk.

DELIBERATE SELF-INFLICTED HARM

Deliberate self-harm or self-injury (also referred to as self-mutilating behavior) in the form of cutting, burning, or scratching is a disturbing form of behavior that may be fairly prevalent among college students (Gratz, Conrad, & Roemer, 2002; White et al., 2002). Because it is a form of behavior that is not likely to be apparent to anyone unless the self-harming student tells someone that she or he engages in this behavior, there are not necessarily clear signs or symptoms to look for. It is possible that certain scars or marks are noticed that raise suspicion, but this does not seem to happen too often because these students will be good at concealing their self-inflicted injuries.

A common way that a student who engages in self-harm will come to the attention of a faculty or staff person is hearing about it from another student. A student may disclose about the behavior to a peer, who in turn feels compelled to say something to someone on campus in a position to intervene. This is frequently how these students come to our attention in the counseling center, but some do seek counseling voluntarily. In fact, there are situations in which someone contacts our office to express concern about a student engaging in self-harm, not realizing that this student is already in counseling. I have found that self-harming behavior tends to be more distressing for others rather than the student who engages in the behavior. Some discussion of the etiology of the behavior will help clarify why this is so.

Though numerous risk factors may be associated with this behavior, the most commonly identified factors are childhood trauma such as physical and/or sexual abuse, and emotional neglect (Gratz et al., 2002; White et al., 2002). The behavior has been understood as a way for people to relieve emotional pain, cope with traumatic memories, reduce emotional numbness, and gain (or regain) a sense of control over one's life and emotions (White et al., 2002). It had been assumed that the behavior was more common among females, but recent evidence suggests that males may be just as prone to engage in deliberate self-harm, with differing risk factors for men and women (e.g., Gratz et al., 2002). This behavior, then, actually represents a way that the individual tries to cope, even though it can be quite disturbing for others if revealed or discovered.

Deliberate self-harm has typically been viewed as a more extreme form of psychopathology. But as I discussed in Chapter 2, this behavior seems to be increasing in prevalence among students who are not necessarily severely disturbed. It is unclear why this might be so, but from what several students have reported to me in counseling sessions, it may be something that is tried as a way to cope with negative events or feelings. Perhaps there is a peer influence dimension to this behavior similar to substance use. In any event, we may continue to see an increase in this type of behavior.

The most important point that needs to be made regarding deliberate self-harm is that students usually engage in the behavior with no intention to commit suicide or die from the behavior. Students who engage in self-cutting, for example, will describe how they cut in less dangerous areas of their bodies or just deep enough to feel the pain but not to do any serious injury requiring medical treatment. Granted, a student could do more serious harm accidentally, but this does not seem to happen that often. Therefore, if it is discovered that a student engages in this type of behavior, there is not necessarily reason to be concerned about any imminent risk or that the student is suicidal. Still, any student doing self-harm is obviously having emotional difficulties and could benefit from counseling intervention.

SUBSTANCE ABUSE

The problem of substance abuse in college students is well documented and continues to receive considerable attention from administrators in higher education. It has been estimated that 20 to 30 percent of students who seek treatment at their campus counseling or mental health center may be engaging in problematic use of alcohol or other drugs (Meilman & Gaylor, 1989). Alcohol has long been the drug of choice among college students with marijuana usually being the second most popular drug (Meilman, Gaylor, Turco, & Stone, 1990). It is not unusual to find college students using an assortment of other drugs as well, including cocaine, ecstasy, hallucinogens, and heroin. Some students abuse prescription medications such as Ritalin and over-the-counter cough medicines that contain codeine. Though less serious, we should probably not overlook the potential for overuse of nicotine and caffeine. Substance abuse of any type can be a contributor to or a symptom of many of the problems experienced by students, such as anxiety, depression, and suicidal behavior. In essence, students may use alcohol or drugs as a way to self-medicate their problems. Even when students are prescribed psychotropic medication they may continue to rely on alcohol or other drugs, which can offset the effect of the medicine.

Alcohol use, binge drinking, and alcohol-related problems remain the primary concern on most college campuses. Strong evidence shows that a significant proportion of students consume alcohol frequently and in large quantities (Clements, 1999; Meilman, Presley, & Cashin, 1997; Meilman, Stone, Gaylor, & Truco, 1990; Steenbarger, 1998), with reported prevalence estimates ranging from 26 to nearly 35 percent of general student samples (Clements, 1999). Students tend to view alcohol use as a vehicle for social activity and sexual opportunity (Meilman & Gaylor, 1989), but it can result in a number of adverse consequences and secondhand effects on college campuses. Examples include unwanted sex, disorderly conduct, property damage, accidents, injuries, violence, and disturbance to others (Steenbarger, 1998; Wechsler, Davenport, Dowdall, Moeykens, & Castillo, 1994; Wechsler, Lee, Kuo, & Lee, 2000).

Researchers have identified specific demographic risk factors for alcohol abuse in college students. Male students have been found to consume more alcohol, drink more frequently, and engage in more binge drinking than female students (Clements, 1999; Steenbarger, 1998). White students have been found to drink more frequently and consume larger quantities of alcohol than non-white students (Clements, 1999; Engs, Diebold, & Hanson, 1994). Student-athletes and members of Greek organizations appear to be particularly at risk for alcohol abuse (Cashin, Presley, and Meilman, 1998; Leichliter, Meilman, Presley, & Cashin, 1998), with the highest risk being associated with the combination of athletic participation and Greek membership (Meilman, Leichliter, & Presley, 1999). Though Greek life may be strongly associated with alcohol abuse, significant alcohol abuse and related problems are found at colleges with limited presence of Greek life (Juhnke, Schroat, Cashwell, & Gmutza, 2003).

Because of the prevalence of alcohol use among students, it can be difficult to differentiate normal social drinkers from the more problematic users. In some cases direct evidence might indicate more problematic use of alcohol, for example, obvious signs of intoxication such as slurred speech, lack of coordination, and smell of alcohol, particularly if observed at atypical hours or at nonalcohol events. Other observable indicators that might suggest alcohol abuse include frequent drowsiness or sleepiness, noticeable changes in personal hygiene care, poor attitudes about studying or other responsibilities, severe mood swings or depression, and noticeable changes in personality. Academic problems such as missing classes and decreased grades are likely to be observed as well.

The signs of alcohol abuse apply to other forms of substance abuse, though symptoms will vary depending on the specific drug or combination of drugs being used. Usually several observable symptoms are required to warrant suspicion of alcohol or drug abuse. Indicators to look for include a dreamy or blank expression, unresponsiveness or wandering mind, watery eyes, giggling and silliness, and noticeable problems in speech (slurred, rapid, or incoherent). Behavior problems such as aggression and violence, dishonesty, and legal troubles (e.g., DUI, possession, theft) are often associated with substance abuse. Certain types of substance abuse (e.g., hallucinogens) might make someone appear psychotic because of confused thinking, paranoia, feelings of detachment, inappropriate affect, or hallucinations.

Substance abuse can be quite disruptive to academic performance (Kessler et al., 1995; Svanum & Zody, 2001). Often this is due to poor attendance and failure to complete assignments on time. Academic-related problems can often be the way that student substance abuse becomes suspected. On the other hand, I have known students who engage in heavy alcohol or drug use without ever having any significant disruption in their academics. In my experience, most cases of substance abuse will interfere with academics, but there are certainly some exceptions. One student who comes to mind managed to maintain a solid grade point average despite smoking marijuana two or three times every day. This student also functioned relatively well in most other respects but relied on the drug to help manage underlying anxiety.

Substance-abusing students may come to our attention as a result of a crisis situation, including legal, medical, or psychological crises. For example, a student may be arrested and charged with possession or distribution, or experience serious medical symptoms related to the alcohol or drug use. One type of situation that a faculty or staff member could encounter would be a student in distress due to intense anxiety or depression associated with drug use or a drug-induced psychotic episode (e.g., hallucinations, delusions). It is important to keep in mind that substance abuse can be at the root of a student's distress even though this will not always be apparent unless the student voluntarily discloses about alcohol or drug use.

EATING DISORDERS

Eating disorders have become a major mental health concern on college campuses, particularly for female undergraduates. A significant number of college women engage in unhealthy weight control behaviors (Mintz & Betz, 1988), with sorority membership being associated with increased risk for disordered eating (Prouty, Protinsky, & Canady, 2002; Schulken, Pinciaro, Sawyer, Jensen, & Hoban, 1997). Although eating disorders are typically observed in women, they may occur among college men more often than previously estimated (Nelson, Hughes, Katz, & Searight, 1999).

Problems related to eating behavior in college students can range from relatively normal but unhealthy eating habits (not uncommon for students) to severe cases of disordered eating. Generally speaking, cases of disordered eating usually involve an excessive concern with one's appearance, weight, and body size. Moreover, one's body image is likely to be distorted. A number of underlying emotional, interpersonal, and personality factors can contribute to disordered eating, such as depression, obsessive-compulsive habits, perfectionism, social anxiety, and dependent personality traits. In addition, sociocultural pressures (to be thin) may be present as well, particularly for young women.

Anorexia and bulimia are the two primary categories of eating disorders commonly observed in college students. Although they have distinct features, they are not mutually exclusive. A student may display varying characteristics of both disorders, sometimes referred to as bulimarexia.

Anorexia

Anorexic students will have an intense fear of eating and see themselves as overweight despite being extremely thin. In addition to a significant weight loss (not due to medical illness), other classic warning signs of anorexia are a severe restricting of diet, frequent denial of being hungry, irrational concerns expressed about gaining weight or being fat, hyperactivity, including excessive exercise, and unusual eating-related rituals (e.g., cutting food into tiny pieces). Other visible indicators result from poor nutrition and weight loss, such as dry skin, hair loss or thinning, and sensitivity to cold even in warm temperatures. Anorexics will often wear baggy clothing to try to conceal what they perceive as being fat. Another potential indicator specifically for female students is a cessation of their menstrual cycle.

The most commonly expressed concern I hear from others on campus about a student possibly being anorexic is that the student appears to be extremely underweight. Of course, this can be one of the most telling signs of anorexia, but we need to remember that being thin is not always a sign of an eating disorder. Similarly, a significant weight loss could be a sign of something other than anorexia, such as illness or depression. The point is not to overreact just on the basis of someone appearing very thin. I have had many students referred to me for counseling by others who suspected them of having an eating disorder because of their appearance or eating habits, but sometimes reasons other than disordered eating explain why they are under-weight or not eating well.

Bulimia

As with anorexia, a person with bulimia will be excessively con-cerned with body weight and appearance. Unlike anorexia, bulimia typically involves a cycle of binge eating and purging behavior. A person with bulimia will have a tendency to eat in an uncontrolled manner and then attempt to eliminate the food through self-induced vomiting, compulsive exercise, or use of laxatives or diuretics. Some-one who engages in this type of behavior may show physical symp-toms such as loss of tooth enamel, broken blood vessels in the face, paleness, swollen glands under the jaw, and darkened circles under the eyes. They may seem moody or irritable and report somatic com-plaints such as stomach or gastrointestinal discomfort, headaches, toothaches, dizziness and feeling faint, and muscle cramps.

Bulimics try to remain secretive about their bingeing or purging but may inadvertently give clues; for example, they may be observed hoarding food, overeating (without any noticeable weight gain), and frequently going to the bathroom immediately after eating. Bulimics have also been known to revert to shoplifting of food, laxatives, and/or items neither wanted nor needed, and may steal food from friends or roommates. There may also be some degree of avoidance of social events and withdrawal from others because of the secretive nature of the behavior.

PSYCHOTIC BEHAVIOR

Symptoms of a psychotic disorder such as schizophrenia are likely to first emerge during the college years, though the numbers of col-lege students who are diagnosed with these disorders are relatively small compared with other types of mental health problems. Encoun-tering a student who displays psychotic behavior is unnerving and can even cause discomfort for mental health professionals. Psychotic symptoms can manifest in various forms: disorganized speech and behavior, paranoid or delusional thoughts, bizarre thoughts or beliefs, auditory hallucinations, and flat or inappropriate affect. Psychotic symptoms, however, are not always indicative of a psychotic disorder; sometimes they are due to mood disorders, obsessive-compulsive disorder (i.e., obsessive thoughts that may seem strange or irrational), substance abuse, or medication use. Regardless of their etiology, psychotic behaviors are confusing, disturbing, anxiety producing, and difficult to respond to.

In the simplest terms, psychotic behavior or episodes occur when a person loses touch with reality or experiences a disturbance in thought. Some of the more common symptoms that might be observed in college students are fragmented, rambling, or incoherent speech and unusual or disjointed thoughts. Affect or emotions may seem flat, blunted, inappropriate, exaggerated, or labile (i.e., abnormal shifting such as going back and forth between laughing and crying). Other observable indicators might be related to the person's appearance such as inappropriate attire, avoidance of any eye contact or prolonged direct eye contact, and poor hygiene. Of course, some of these variables may be due to other factors, and it can be especially difficult to evaluate certain aspects of appearance in college students. As an example, I often see students wearing what might be considered inappropriate clothing such as shorts during the winter and wool caps in the summer. Some of these behaviors may be more indicative of wanting to be different or drawing attention to oneself, or perhaps just being somewhat eccentric in personality. Thus, we must use caution when interpreting student appearance and behavior as indicating something about their state of mind.

Students who experience paranoia and delusions are particularly challenging to evaluate, depending on the nature of their fears or delusions. When the delusions are bizarre, there will usually be no doubt about the fact that they are indeed delusions. I remember seeing a student, for example, who thought that the water cooler in his psychiatrist's office contained poison. When the delusions are not so bizarre, there may be less certainty about whether they are grounded in reality. A few of the most common nonbizarre delusions are ones that involve fears of being followed or deceived, grandiosity (i.e., inflated sense of identity, self-worth, knowledge, ability, etc.), and somatic (i.e., belief that one has some type of physical defect or medical illness despite absence of medical evidence).

Delusions associated with dating and romantic relationships can be especially difficult to assess. I see so many students who seem overly sensitive and suspicious about the prospect of a romantic partner cheating on them that the line becomes blurred between normal developmentally based behavior and jealousy that might border on paranoia. I have also had some experiences in which students talk about the prospect of having or actually having a relationship with someone, only to eventually discover that this is primarily a fantasy or more imagined than real.

Psychotic symptoms are likely to cause a disruption in academic functioning. However, in some instances students may experience delusions or other psychotic symptoms without interference to their ability to study and perform well academically. Arnstein (1989) presented an example of a student who had delusions about other students making fun of him as well as auditory hallucinations, but without any impairment to his intellectual functioning; indeed, this student apparently had an improvement in grades because his delusions made him isolate himself and spend more time studying. However, psychotic symptoms or a psychotic episode will likely incapacitate most students until they receive proper treatment.

SUMMARY

It can be important for college personnel to recognize potential signs and symptoms of specific types of problems commonly observed in the college student population. Some of the most commonly observed problems are anxiety, depression, deliberate self-inflicted harm, alcohol and drug abuse, eating disorders, and psychotic behavior. Noncounseling college personnel do not need to diagnose specific problems per se but should be able to at least recognize signs of certain forms of student distress. Being able to do so can help in the process of ensuring that students receive proper mental health care.

Chapter 4

Approaching a Student
with Your Concerns

In Chapters 2 and 3, I described signs and symptoms to indicate that a student might be experiencing emotional or psychological difficulties. In this chapter, I offer some suggestions for intervening with a student you suspect is experiencing some type of distress. These suggestions are primarily for situations in which you are willing to approach a student based on your concerns. Much of the material in this chapter is drawn from my experiences consulting with others in the campus community and includes suggestions that have been most helpful for others in intervening with emotionally troubled students. The process of approaching a student can be relatively straightforward or more challenging and complex depending on a number of variables. Although every situation has unique elements, college personnel should be aware of some general principles of intervention.

Understandably some faculty and staff members are not comfortable attempting to approach troubled students and may prefer to consult with and arrange for others, such as campus counselors, to intervene (this process is discussed in Chapter 5). However, there may be times when you will not be able to avoid having to deal directly with a student in distress. For instance, if a student becomes upset or voluntarily discloses about personal problems while meeting with you, some degree of *intervention* will be required. Remember that the term intervention here simply refers to the process of taking an initial step designed to help a student find proper care and services when needed.

For noncounselors on campus, approaching a student whose behavior or comments have aroused concern can be anxiety provoking. You may have fears that the student will respond in a negative manner, especially when the student has not initiated discussion about his

College Students in Distress
© 2006 by The Haworth Press, Inc. All rights reserved.
doi:10.1300/5228_04

or her problems. When a student is the initiator, it is easy for you to then express concern or ask questions. As an example, imagine you are meeting with a student who makes references to personal issues that are causing some disruption in the student's academics. With some brief exploration, you will likely be able to get a sense of how much the student is in distress and what help, if any, the student is receiving. In contrast, when you are the one to initiate the intervention, you may feel like you are being too intrusive and venturing into unknown territory.

I believe it is appropriate for you as a faculty or staff member to approach a student in most situations when you have concerns about the student's emotional or psychological well-being. One exception is when you are concerned that a student might be at risk of harm to oneself or others. If a student has conveyed any hint of suicide risk, I strongly recommend consulting with a counselor first if possible. Situations involving concern about potential suicide risk before you have an opportunity to consult with a counselor are discussed later in this chapter. When dealing with threats of harm to others, you could consult with either the counseling center or dean of students office or go directly to the campus police or public safety office if you believe there is imminent danger (e.g., a clear threat made against any identified persons). For situations in which a student discloses being the victim of an assault or rape, or is being stalked or threatened in any way, try to encourage without overly pressuring the student to contact the campus police; also refer the student to either the counseling office or another resource (e.g., dean of students, health center, women's center) that will provide support and explore the student's options.

As mentioned earlier, it is generally preferred to err on the side of overreaction when you are concerned about a student. Usually the worst outcome is that the student feels somewhat embarrassed or becomes a little defensive, but this is worth the risk if it helps prevent a student from subsequently experiencing problems of a more serious magnitude. I have witnessed many situations in which people on campus waited far too long before intervening or seeking help regarding a student they were concerned about, and the matter became more troublesome. Many students will actually respond positively when they learn that others are attending to them or noticing that they are struggling, even if it turns out that the problems are not as serious as imagined. Early intervention can help reduce the chance of a student's problems turning into a crisis situation later on.

GENERAL GUIDELINES FOR INTERVENTION

When you are concerned about a student's emotional or psychological well-being, a few general guidelines may be helpful to follow if you choose to approach the student before consulting with a campus counselor.

The Right Time and Place

First and foremost, it is important to approach a student at an appropriate time and in an appropriate place. You want to speak to the student when others are not present, and therefore you may need to initially approach the student with a gentle, "I need a chance to speak with you. Can we schedule a time to meet?" If possible, do this when you have some free time, allowing for the possibility to meet at that moment if the student's schedule permits. In general, try to arrange to meet as soon as possible to lessen the prospect of the student forgetting or otherwise missing the appointment. Give the student your telephone number to call and/or ask for the student's number (preferably a cell phone number if available) in the event the appointment is not or cannot be kept as scheduled. I find that this can lessen the probability of the student failing to keep the appointment because it serves not only as a reminder but a clear indication that it is important. This will also allow you to contact the student if he or she fails to keep the appointment without calling to notify you.

Once an appropriate time and place is established, you can then present your concerns in a manner that feels safe and nonthreatening to the student. You may not have complete control over aspects of the room or office where you choose to meet the student, but it is preferable to have privacy with no distractions or interruptions. It is helpful to have a telephone available for contacting other offices on campus as needed, and the numbers should be readily available on a resource list or in a telephone directory. You want to avoid answering any unrelated calls if possible while speaking to the student.

Be Direct (Share Your Observations)

Although you do not want to be perceived as confrontational or punitive, it is also important not to be too tentative or cautious when speaking with a student. Saying what needs to be said in a direct manner is generally the best way to proceed. You should be specific about the student's behaviors or comments that aroused your concern. For instance, if you have observed a noticeable change in a student's behavior that suggests that the student may be depressed, present what you have observed (e.g., "Lately I have noticed that you appear sad and withdrawn, and you have been falling asleep in my class"). This is preferable to general comments such as "you seem depressed," which could be easily dismissed or denied. In general you want to avoid doing guesswork or trying to render diagnoses, even tentatively. Instead, observations of specific behaviors may not be easily disregarded and can help make students aware of problems they are experiencing.

Be frank with a student but try not to pressure a student into admitting having a specific type of problem. I remember a case involving a coach who was convinced that a student had an eating disorder and persisted in trying to get the student to acknowledge it. As it turned out, the student actually suffered from severe anxiety and gastrointestinal symptoms that limited her appetite and caused her to severely restrict her diet. Because of her eating-related symptoms and the fact that she was thin, it was understandable that someone might suspect the student of having an eating disorder. But the coach was so convinced that she referred the student for counseling and insisted that she see someone who specialized in treating eating disorders.

While it is important to recognize symptoms of specific problems such as eating disorders, it is not necessary to diagnose student problems per se in order to facilitate a referral. Most campus counselors are generalists who can work with any student problem and if appropriate can arrange for students to see colleagues who may have special expertise with certain types of problems. Even if your diagnosis is accurate, it can still backfire if you try to get a student to admit having a specific type of problem because the student may be in denial, lack awareness, or not be ready to acknowledge a problem.

Another issue to consider is what to say when you decide to approach a student on the basis of information obtained from other students. In many instances you could easily approach the student with your concerns without having to reveal the source of information, especially if you were in position to make these observations yourself. However, if the observations could have come only from others, then you will probably need to reveal this. At the same time you may need to be protective of the identity of other students unless they give permission for you to reveal their names. The ideal situation is when you have this permission, but this will not always be the case.

I am often faced with this quandary in my role as a college counselor. Students come to me with concerns about a fellow student without wanting me to tell the student that they have spoken to me. Even parents sometimes call with concerns but do not want their children to know that they called. Sometimes you have to be creative in letting a student know that concerns have been expressed without revealing any specific sources. I imagine that students are sometimes smart enough to figure out who may have prompted the concern about them even when we do not reveal specific names. Again, the student may be angry or upset about others prompting concern, but this is better than not taking any action if the student is having serious problems.

Express Concern

Counselors are generally well trained in how to demonstrate empathy and compassion through both verbal and nonverbal means, but this capacity will vary greatly among noncounselors on a college campus. Although being empathic may come naturally for some, it is not essential to be able to demonstrate or convey empathy. *Empathy* is generally defined as the ability to understand what another person is feeling or experiencing almost as if you are putting yourself in the other person's situation. Empathy is a complex process that can be difficult to truly experience. The most important aspect is to be able to verbalize concern for a student's well-being. This may be as simple as prefacing your comments or observations with "I am concerned about how you are doing and want to make sure that you are okay." As much as possible you want to convey to the student that you are concerned and supportive yet nonjudgmental. It can be challenging for some people to refrain from coming across as judgmental or punitive, especially for certain types of behavior (e.g., substance abuse), but students will be more willing to open up or share honestly about what they are experiencing when they do not need to fear being judged in any way.

It is also important not to minimize what may be going on with the student, regardless of how it might appear. Sometimes people unwittingly minimize or dismiss a student's distress in an effort to make the student feel better. A good example of this is the student who gets extremely anxious about taking exams even though he or she generally performs well academically. Others are likely to respond to the student's anxiety with reassurances such as "I am sure you will do fine" or "You have nothing to worry about." Such comments may seem logical given the student's history of strong academic performance, but they will not help reduce the student's anxiety. It would be better to acknowledge the difficulty with anxiety and recommend that the student seek assistance to help manage it.

Ask About Current or Past Use of Counseling

When approaching a student that you are concerned about, be prepared to ask some specific questions related to the student's current and past use of counseling. A few simple questions might prove useful in determining the student's receptiveness to a referral for counseling. If the student acknowledges that he or she is having emotional or psychological problems, do not feel as if you need to go into much detail or acquire a lot of information. The most important thing is to find out whether the student has sought any type of assistance for the problems.

You will find that in some cases the student is already getting help through counseling either on or off campus. For students that are not currently in counseling, you want to see if they have ever used counseling, whether on campus or elsewhere. Students who have used counseling before might be more open to the idea of trying it again unless they had a negative experience with it. In a sense what you are trying to do is assess the student's willingness to use counseling services (particularly on campus) because your main objective will be to make a referral. If the student is not already in counseling and seems resistant to the idea, then you should consult with someone in the counseling office after speaking with the student. You may still want to consult with the counseling office even if the student informs you that he or she is already in counseling. This is because you may be concerned that the student's counselor is not aware of something or could otherwise benefit from your information.

SPECIFIC SCENARIOS

There are a number of specific scenarios involving troubled students that you might be faced with at some point. Because these situations can be unsettling for noncounseling personnel, I will devote some attention to a few of the more common ones.

Crying Student

As a counselor for many years, I have become well accustomed to students crying. Aside from making sure that I always have a box of tissues handy, I do not feel compelled to do anything other than what I usually do when a student cries or displays strong emotions. I certainly do not feel any need for the student to stop crying. But for the noncounselor, sitting with a crying student may feel awkward or uncomfortable, and there may be a greater sense of urgency and need to do something to stop the crying. Sometimes I receive calls from others on campus who express concern about a student crying even though they are not clear as to *why* the student is crying. For some people the crying is enough to trigger an alarm. Although we should consider crying a clear sign of distress, we should not assume the worst just on the basis of a student crying. Crying is not always an accurate barometer of the degree of someone's distress. Some students cry quite easily over relatively minor issues, whereas others will not cry even when they talk about painful or emotionally distressing events. But crying can somehow make it seem as if a student is in severe distress because it is such a visible sign of emotion.

Some students will begin to cry when you first approach them with your concerns. You may also find yourself in a situation in which a student starts to cry during a meeting or other context. For example, faculty members will sometimes have this happen when students come to see them about doing poorly in their class. When dealing with a crying student, the key is whether the student is verbal and can talk about what is upsetting or prompting the crying. If the student is able or willing to talk, then you can use the suggestions provided earlier in this chapter. Try not to feel too anxious just because the student is crying.

With a crying student who is not verbal, it is difficult to respond because the student does not (or cannot) verbalize what is causing the distress. It can leave you feeling helpless or powerless to do anything to help. In this situation, patience and persistence will be required. I have had crisis intervention sessions in which it took nearly thirty minutes or more just to find out why the student was upset. It will likely be more challenging for the noncounselor to sit with a distressed but nonverbal student for that long; therefore, it might be necessary to call for assistance early on if this is the case.

Angry Student

Similar to a crying student, a student who is angry or agitated can cause discomfort for others. Some people who work on college campuses, such as those who work in the registrar's or bursar's office, routinely deal with angry students. In some ways, dealing with an angry student is similar to handling customer relations in a business. Depending on the nature of your concerns, the personality of the student, and your role on campus, a student could potentially react with anger when first approached. As much as possible, try not to personalize the student's anger because it is highly likely to be misdirected and not necessarily meant to be aimed at you in particular. For example, a student who is experiencing problems may be on edge and easily provoked to anger or defensiveness.

When responding to an angry student, remain calm and try to keep the student calm. If a student reacts angrily to your expressing concern and challenges your observations or reports from others, simply inform the student that as a university employee you have an obligation to reach out to students who may be having problems and that you are concerned about the student's welfare. Sometimes students react with anger because they think that they are going to get into trouble or maybe even kicked out of college. Thus, it might also be helpful to reassure a student that that is not your intent. If a student continues to be agitated, allow the student to leave once you have voiced your concerns and then take the next step of consulting with the counseling office. In the rare instance of a student becoming overtly threatening in any way, you should report this to the campus police or first consult with someone else on campus on how to handle the situation.

Student Behaving Strangely

Another situation that can be especially disconcerting is intervening with a student who behaves in a strange manner, either verbally or nonverbally. This can take many forms. There might be something strange about a student's appearance or behavior, such as a student who makes bizarre or incoherent comments. You may want to consult with a campus counselor prior to intervening when unusual behavior is observed, although you might end up having to interact in some capacity with the student before you have a chance to consult with anyone.

Perhaps second only to calls about students believed to be at risk for suicide or self-harm are calls we receive about students who display strange behavior or make unusual comments. In such cases we will typically receive numerous calls from various people on campus regarding an individual student. Although unusual behavior can be quite disturbing, there is not necessarily any urgency unless the student makes comments that suggest a degree of risk to self or others. The most that you can do is be as responsive to the student as you can and avoid pretending to understand something that the student says that does not make sense to you. You may want to express concern that you are having difficulty following what the student is telling you and this can be used as an opportunity to enlist the assistance of another person on campus. Particularly when there is concern about a student not being oriented to reality, someone from the counseling office will likely need to conduct a mental status exam (which is used primarily to diagnose psychosis and other severe psychological disorders).

Student Having a Panic Attack

Because of the physiological symptoms, a student having a panic attack is likely to first seek assistance at the health center on campus. If the attack occurs after regular operating hours for the campus, the student may even go to a hospital emergency room, particularly if this is a first full-blown attack. Occasionally a student will have a panic attack while in the office of a faculty or staff member. I have received some calls over the years to respond to such situations.

When a student is having a panic episode, it can be difficult to refer the student to a counselor because the student may be convinced that it is some type of medical or physical problem. If you are with a student who appears to be having a panic attack, it can be helpful just to maintain a calm and reassuring presence. Even though medical intervention is not required for a panic attack, it is still wise to use medical personnel, particularly if there is any doubt or uncertainty about the nature of what the student is experiencing (e.g., could it be a seizure or reaction to medication?). It will also be reassuring for the student to have a medical practitioner present. If it is ultimately determined that it was a panic attack, the medical professional can then refer the student to counseling, which is typically what happens with panic attack patients who go to hospital emergency rooms.

Student Making References to Suicide

As discussed earlier, it is best to consult with someone in the counseling office or perhaps the dean of students office whenever you suspect a student might be at risk for suicide. However, you may find yourself in a situation where you must respond to a student's comments that suggest potential risk for suicide. As an example, I recently consulted with a professor who was concerned about a student who came to see her after missing class a few times. Apparently the student made comments about having a number of personal problems and generally appeared to be in significant distress. While talking with the professor, the student made a comment that he would have killed himself over the weekend if he had had the pills to do it. Naturally the professor was alarmed by his comment. The professor tried to refer the student over to the counseling office, but he was strongly against counseling. She was unsure what to do after that and eventually let the student leave, whereupon she called our office.

The professor did the right thing by trying to arrange for the student to be evaluated by someone in the counseling center. But given the student's resistance to the idea, she did not know what to do next. It was appropriate for the professor to let the student leave and then contact our office. The only other thing she could have done would have been to tell the student that she had an obligation to consult with others because of the student's comment and reluctance to see a counselor. Because she did not inform the student as such, he reacted with anger when I subsequently called him in his residence. He was angry that the professor contacted our office, although at some level he had to know that she needed to take some type of action. Though angry about it initially, he eventually became more receptive to seeing someone in our office and was eventually seen for an evaluation.

Thus, it is important to keep in mind that anytime students make comments or references to suicide, there is an obligation to do something. The ideal situation is when students agree to allow you to arrange for them to see a counselor at that moment. When students are not agreeable as such, then you should inform them that you have an obligation to consult with someone in the counseling or dean of students office. Do not agree or promise to keep students' comments confidential when they might be at risk. Granted, students may get angry or upset with you, but they need to know that you are not in a position to maintain confidentiality when you have concerns about suicide risk. It is best if students know right up front about this rather than get an unexpected call from someone later on. The student in the situation I described may have felt somewhat betrayed by the professor calling the counseling center. Sometimes when you tell a student that you need to consult with someone because of your concern, the student may acquiesce and show some understanding about your need to do so.

In cases in which students' comments are not explicit but make you suspect suicide, then you may need to at least express your concern that they may be at risk based on the comments made. Do not avoid using the term *suicide* when speaking to students (e.g., ask students if they are experiencing thoughts about suicide). There is a persistent myth that talking about suicide will plant the idea in a student's mind, and belief in this myth can make people hesitant to talk about suicide in a direct manner. You should not be afraid to use the term, as it will actually be helpful and relieving for most students who may be experiencing suicidal thoughts to acknowledge them. It may be frightening to imagine a student acknowledging suicidal thoughts or intentions because you may not know what to say or ask at that point. An acknowledgment of suicidal thoughts or intentions is enough for you to refer students for further evaluation and gives you justification for consulting with the counseling office when students are unwilling to meet with a counselor. You should not place yourself in the position of having to do a suicide risk assessment.

If you express concern to a student that he or she may be at risk based on something that was said and the student then denies any suicidal ideation or intentions, you should still consider consulting with someone in the counseling office to determine if any other action needs to be taken. This will shift the burden of responsibility to the people who are supposed to make such judgment calls and alleviate your own anxiety or doubt about what else if anything should be done. Also, remember to have emergency numbers handy for situations that occur after regular working hours (emergency procedures and after-hours crises are addressed in Chapter 7).

Student Conveying Distress in Written Form

The situation can be a little trickier when students give indications of being in distress through some type of written format. The most common scenario is when students do this through electronic mail, but it can also happen through writing assignments, handwritten notes, and even on exams. If a student writes something that explicitly or implicitly suggests suicide, I recommend that you consult with a campus counselor as soon as possible. Of course, the counselor will need to know the specific references or comments written by the student, and in cases of assigned material it might be necessary for the counselor to read the entire paper in order to evaluate specific comments within the context of the assignment.

Written expressions of distress that do not indicate suicide should be handled similarly to concerns about a student based on observations or reports from others. You could still choose to consult with someone first, but it would be appropriate to approach students to talk about what was written and determine if they are getting help or are receptive to getting help. In my experience, when students use assignments or other opportunities to convey their distress or despair through writing, this is usually a way that they are seeking attention from others. Few students would be surprised by efforts to reach out to them based on written expressions of distress.

SUMMARY

Faculty and staff members are often in a good position to approach students who arouse concern. There are some general principles for how college personnel can initially intervene and present their concerns to students. Although some noncounseling personnel may choose to consult with the counseling office rather than approach a student, there may be situations that do not allow for consultation before responding to a student in distress.

Chapter 5

The Referral Process

It has been suggested by Archer (1991) that noncounselors on campus can learn to use basic counseling skills and serve in counseling-like roles with students whose problems are situational or developmental in nature. Archer advocated this as a way to alleviate pressure on counseling centers with limited resources and as an alternative for students who are unlikely to seek professional help. Although Archer was clear about the need for noncounselors to know their limitations and when to refer to a counselor, it is my opinion that it may be too risky for noncounselors to ever attempt to do counseling even on a limited basis. There are two reasons for this. First, student problems that seem situational or developmental initially may later prove to be more serious or chronic. Second, it can be more difficult to refer a student for counseling after serving as a pseudo or surrogate counselor. For example, some students may feel abandoned or rejected in response to subsequent attempts to refer them to someone else. Hence, I recommend that college personnel with no formal counselor training serve primarily as referral agents for students.

Being able to refer distressed or troubled students to counseling is an important skill for faculty and staff members to possess. Not surprisingly, college personnel may have misperceptions and limited knowledge about counseling services on their campus (Bishop, Bishop, & Beale, 1992). To counter this, some counseling centers offer training programs for faculty and staff on how to refer troubled students (Ellingson, Kochenour, & Weitzman, 1999; Rodolfa, 1987), with some designed specifically for disruptive behavior in class (De Lucia & Iasenza, 1995) or problems in the residential setting (Grosz, 1991). Written referral guides for faculty and staff might be distributed by some counseling centers as well (Bishop et al., 1992;

Ellingson et al., 1999; Hernandez & Fister, 2001; Rodolfa, 1987). Additional information on how to refer troubled students is also available for those serving as academic advisors (Allen & Trimble, 1993).

The referral process can range from being quite simple to extremely difficult depending upon the student's openness to professional help. A vast body of literature discusses the factors that can influence college students' willingness to seek professional help, such as demographics, personality traits, and attitudes about seeking help. Some of these factors are addressed in this chapter. Given that numerous factors can play a role in determining students' receptiveness to the idea of counseling, your attempts to refer students may or may not be successful. With some students, the recommendation or suggestion will be enough to prompt them to seek help, whereas others will refuse to go under any circumstances. Still others will appear to be receptive to the suggestion but then fail to follow through. Although problems can emerge at any point in the referral process in spite of your best efforts, you can follow a few general guidelines to help facilitate the process and minimize complications.

Before giving suggestions on how to make a referral, it may be helpful to first have a framework for thinking about the referral process. Though presented many years ago, the conceptualization articulated by Corazzini and Shelton (1974) offers an important perspective for understanding the process. In essence, they suggested that instead of thinking about referring students to counseling as simply passing them on to a more appropriate resource, the process should be viewed as a "transfer of trust." That is, referral agents can provide a bridge to promote trust in the counseling office. This is likely to be easier with students with whom you already have an established positive relationship but can still be done with students you are not as familiar with. Many of the original ideas that underscore the perspective of Corazzini and Shelton are incorporated into the suggestions that follow.

WAYS TO FACILITATE A REFERRAL
TO COUNSELING

The probability of making a successful referral can be significantly enhanced if certain steps are followed. The following suggestions are intended to increase receptiveness to counseling and counter potential negative reactions and resistance. These suggestions apply to situations that do not require immediate action; situations involving a sense of urgency are discussed later in this chapter.

Discussing the Option of Counseling

Generally speaking, the referral process should be viewed as a joint endeavor in which students are active participants in the decision to seek counseling. Students should be allowed to express their concerns, fears, and reservations about counseling and have a sense of freedom of choice. For example, after suggesting counseling, you could then ask, "What do you think of this suggestion?"

If a student inquires about the possibility of seeing you instead of going to a counselor, you need to be clear about limitations in your role which preclude you from helping students with personal problems. You should then inform the student that services are available on campus for that purpose and you would be willing to assist in arranging for the student to meet with a campus counselor. Some students may react negatively, but it is important to maintain this boundary. Imagine how difficult it might be to try to refer the student after you have already been available in that capacity. Some students might interpret this as you seeing their problems to be much more serious than first imagined. Although this would not necessarily be an inappropriate interpretation on their part, it might leave them feeling more distressed about their problems. This is why I have stressed the need to refrain from assuming any type of counseling-like role with students. It is best to keep the boundaries clear from the outset.

When you make the suggestion for counseling, student reactions can vary quite a bit. As alluded to earlier, a number of factors can influence a student's willingness to accept a referral. One critical issue is simply the timing or student's readiness to receive help. Research suggests that people progress through stages toward making a change in their behavior (Prochaska, DiClemente, & Norcross, 1992). This is particularly true for substance abuse but can be applied to most problems. According to this model, students in the initial stage will not even be aware of their problems and thus will have no motivation to seek help. Students may be pressured by others to get into counseling, but few at this stage will benefit from it under coercive conditions.

Some students recognize that they have problems they need to deal with but are not yet ready to take any action. Students further along in the stages of change will be more willing to seek help and may have already begun to take steps on their own.

Attitudes about seeking help can be another important factor to consider. For example, some students may recognize that they need help but are resistant because of negative attitudes associated with receiving professional help (Kahn & Williams, 2003). Reports of increasing numbers of students seeking counseling suggests that help-seeking is less stigmatized than in the past, but a sense of shame or embarrassment may still persist for many students. This may be particularly true for male students. Male students have been found to hold more negative attitudes about seeking help than female students (Kahn & Nauta, 1997; Kelly & Achter, 1995). It has also been found that students who have had prior counseling tend to have more positive attitudes about help-seeking than students who have not had any prior counseling (Deane & Todd, 1996). This is why it can be important to ask about previous counseling as discussed in Chapter 4. In general you may find female students and those with previous counseling experience to be more receptive to a referral.

Preparing Students for What to Expect

When referring students who have not been to the campus counseling center before, it can be helpful to give them some sense of what to expect when they go there for the first time. This will require that you have some degree of familiarity with the counseling services on your campus. Perhaps the most important information that you can provide is about the staff members in the counseling office. Ideally you would get to know most if not all of the staff, which might be realistic on smaller campuses with only one or two counselors but could be difficult on larger campuses that have several counselors on staff. With larger centers it might be important to at least know who serves as the administrative director and clinical services director.

Aside from knowing staff member names, you may want to obtain additional information about the staff such as their credentials and any areas of expertise. The credentials of college counselors will vary somewhat, but the majority are psychologists and professional counselors. Many counseling centers serve as a training site for graduate students in counseling or counseling-related programs, so trainees may be working in the center under the supervision of senior staff members. It might also be important to have a sense of the demographics of the counselors, such as gender and race, because some students may express preferences for counselors they would feel most comfortable talking to. Even counselor demographics such as age, marital status, and religion can be perceived as relevant factors for some students depending on the nature of their problems.

In addition to knowing about the staff, you might want to get a sense of how the counseling center functions. This includes specific information such as operating hours, scheduling of appointments, eligibility for services, and whether any fees are charged. It might be important to inquire about the use of wait-lists, for there may be a waiting period before receiving ongoing counseling for students whose cases are not considered urgent or in need of immediate attention. Some centers, especially on larger campuses, may need to use a wait-list strategy during peak times of demand for counseling. You can also learn about the typical types of concerns students seek help for and what types of services are available. Most centers will have a Web page from which this information can be easily accessed.

Although counseling centers will vary somewhat in terms of the services they provide, almost all will offer individual counseling (typically on a once-a-week basis). However, it is not unusual for centers to impose limits on the number of sessions as a solution to the growing demand for services (Lacour & Carter, 2002). Fortunately, limitations on the number of sessions offered do not appear to deter students from utilizing counseling (Uffelman & Hardin, 2002). Students do not usually have a specific time frame in mind for counseling, and many may actually prefer to use counseling on a short-term basis (i.e., six sessions or less). Some centers may see students only for evaluations or very short-term counseling and then make referrals to outside agencies or service providers with whom the school has contracted.

Many counseling centers will offer group, in addition to, individual counseling. Group counseling is usually offered in a general format for students with any type of problem or using a theme-oriented approach for students with specific types of problems. Group counseling can be particularly effective for students with interpersonal, social, or relationship difficulties. Support groups for specific populations of students such as gay, lesbian, and bisexual students might be available as well.

You may also want to be aware of what is available to students in terms of psychiatric services. Students may inquire specifically about the availability of medication as an option for treatment. Most counseling centers will be prepared to respond to the need for students to be evaluated for psychotropic medication use. Because of the growing need for this type of service, many centers now provide psychiatric consultation on site, but if not they will refer students to appropriate off-campus resources.

It can also be helpful to know something about the process when a student goes to the counseling center for the first time. Although there can be some variation in this process, there are procedures that most centers share in common. Students are usually asked to complete intake forms when they have their first appointment. At the very least, this usually consists of an informed consent form and a basic information form (demographics, information about previous counseling, etc.). Some centers may also include a measure used to assess the student's current level of symptom distress. It is important to note, however, that students are not usually asked to complete forms if they are experiencing a high level of distress, for example, when a student is seen for a crisis intervention session.

After intake forms are completed, the student will meet with a staff member for an initial session lasting about fifty minutes to an hour. The counselor will use this first session to obtain information about the student's presenting problems and level of distress. Questions may be asked routinely about family background, alcohol and drug use, suicidal ideation and behavior, academic and social functioning, and other important aspects of the student's life. Counselors understand that some students are uncomfortable with this process of information gathering and do their best to obtain critical information in a sensitive and respectful manner.

One of the most important aspects of counseling that should be mentioned to a student when you try to make a referral is the principle of confidentiality. Some students may be especially inquisitive about the confidentiality of counseling, particularly if they have never been in counseling before. When discussing this issue with a student, the key is to reassure the student that what is discussed with a counselor remains confidential but without giving the impression that it is absolute. The reason for this is that there are limits to confidentiality. The one exception to confidentiality that is most likely to emerge is when a student is deemed to be a danger to self or others. Although relatively rare, in certain situations counselors may need to break confidentiality in order to protect a student who threatens suicide or protect someone a student threatens to harm. In most cases, informing a student about this limit to confidentiality will not be an issue or deterrent when trying to refer the student to counseling.

Creating a Favorable Mind-Set

When referring a student it can be facilitative to establish positive expectations for counseling. As much as possible you want to convey a positive attitude and sense of confidence in the counseling services on your campus. It can be especially helpful if you are able to make a referral to someone you recommend, as this will convey a sense of confidence in this particular person. Of course, this should be an honest and accurate belief in this person's ability to help students and not just a way to convince a student to see someone. Again, this is why it can be important to be familiar with at least a couple of staff members in the counseling center, and ideally these would be people you feel comfortable referring students to.

When making a personal referral you could say something such as the following: "Dr. Sharkin has helped many students with problems similar to what you are experiencing, and I think that you will feel comfortable talking to him. I am confident that he can be of help to you." Expressing this kind of confidence in a specific person can have a positive influence on a student's willingness to accept a referral. It might simply be reassuring for a student to seek help from someone who has been recommended. You can still be effective as a referral agent without necessarily being familiar with any of the counselors, but it can be an advantage in certain cases to be able to refer to a specific individual.

Some students will respond with apprehensiveness about the idea of counseling largely due to misperceptions or misunderstandings about counseling. Also, as noted earlier, students may experience a sense of shame and stigma associated with getting professional help. For example, use of counseling may be perceived as a sign of weakness or indication of serious disturbance in one's mental health. You should not be surprised to encounter some strong negative reactions from students in response to the suggestion of counseling. Some students may actually hear your suggestion as implying that you think they are crazy. Students can be quite sensitive to the way they are perceived by others, and a referral for counseling can be interpreted (or misinterpreted) in funny ways.

In response to students who seem to struggle with negative associations to counseling (particularly if based on faulty notions or misinformation), you can alleviate any irrational fears by dispelling myths and normalizing counseling. You can characterize counseling as helpful for students dealing with all types of everyday difficulties and not just for those with more serious problems. It may also be reassuring to characterize going for counseling as a sign of strength rather than weakness. Although it is appropriate to validate a student's anxiety about going to a counselor for the first time as normal and understandable, you want to try to instill a sense of counseling as something that is likely to provide relief from distress for the student.

It is possible that students who have been in counseling before will be resistant because they may have had a negative experience with it. For some students the previous experience may have occurred years ago; perhaps they were coerced into seeing a mental health professional during their childhood or earlier adolescent years. When faced with trying to refer students who reveal having had negative prior experiences with counseling, the most you can do is acknowledge their reservations as understandable but be encouraging of them trying it again, especially given that it might feel different to do so under different circumstances (e.g., no coercion, being older).

The most troublesome situation is when a student reveals having already made an attempt to see a counselor on campus but characterizes it as a negative or unhelpful experience. In this case, you should encourage the student to give it another try with a different counselor, noting that sometimes there are mismatches between students and counselors or other factors that make the first attempt unsuccessful. You can tell students that it is not uncommon for this to happen and that students sometimes need to specifically request to meet with a different counselor than before. This can also be another opportunity to make a personal referral to someone you recommend (assuming it is not the counselor whom the student already met with).

Because it can be important to establish positive expectations when making a referral, you might want to take a moment to reflect on your own attitudes and potential biases regarding help-seeking and counseling. Faculty and staff members are likely to vary widely in their attitudes and beliefs about counseling and some are more likely to make referrals than others. Men may be generally less inclined than women to refer others for counseling (regardless of the referral recipient's gender) (Lott, Ness, Alcorn, & Greer, 1999), and female faculty members in particular may be more likely than their male counterparts to make referrals for certain types of problems such as depression and eating disorders (Backels & Wheeler, 2001). If you hold negative ideas about help-seeking or lack confidence in the effectiveness of counseling, it is perhaps unlikely that you will suggest counseling to students unless you are very concerned about their well-being. However, it may be difficult to convince students to seek help if you are yourself skeptical of professional help because you may somehow inadvertently communicate your own biases to students. The point is that you want to try to keep your own attitudes and beliefs from getting in the way of being able to refer students to counseling when they might benefit from it.

Setting the Stage for Follow-Up

The process of following up on a student you refer to counseling is addressed later in this chapter, but it should be first mentioned here because you can lay the groundwork for follow-up at the time you make the referral. Although it may not be necessary in every case, it can be important to follow up with students that you refer to counseling. Ideally, you would arrange to touch base with a student in a follow-up meeting to see how the student is doing and whether he or she made contact with the counseling office. In some instances, however, you may want to take things a step further by having contact yourself with the counseling office, perhaps just to verify that someone saw the student.

The biggest obstacle in doing follow-up is confidentiality of counseling. You will need to have a student's permission to speak to someone in the counseling office even if it is simply to get confirmation that the student was seen. Thus, when you make a referral, you should discuss this with the student and try to obtain the student's permission for you to follow up on his or her behalf. Convey that this is just to ensure that the student is okay and in the event that you are unable to follow up with the student directly. You will need to instruct the student to sign a release of confidential information consent form at the time of the first appointment, noting that this is often done when faculty and staff members refer students. In most cases this will not be a problem and students will be agreeable to it. If for some reason a student seems hesitant to do this, reassure the student that the only information you will ask for is verification of attendance. With students who seem concerned about privacy and confidentiality, let them know that you want to verify only that they were able to meet with a counselor. The ideal situation is when students give you permission to call the counseling center while they are present when you help arrange for an appointment. Your interest in follow-up can be discussed with someone in the counseling center at that time, ensuring that the counselor who will meet with the student will be made aware that you would like to get verification of the student's attendance.

WHEN THERE IS A SENSE OF URGENCY

Thus far, I have been providing suggestions about how to refer students to counseling when there is no sense of urgency. However, you may be faced with situations in which you believe that students should be seen or evaluated by a counselor as soon as possible. In such cases, you will need to take additional steps in order to ensure that the students receive prompt attention.

Depending on your role on campus or nature of relationship with a particular student, you may have leverage that you can use to make sure that a student is seen for an evaluation session in the counseling office. For example, faculty members often seem to have this type of perceived authority with advisees or students who are currently enrolled in their classes. However, relatively few people on a campus really have the authority to require a student to see a counselor. Two individuals who may have the most authority for this purpose are the dean of students and senior administrative officer in student affairs (or student services). This is important to keep in mind because these individuals may need to be notified in certain cases.

When you have a student with you whom you want to be seen by a counselor right away, ask if the student is willing to allow you to call the counseling center and arrange for an immediate appointment. It is a good sign if the student is agreeable to this, but I have experienced situations in which students do not follow through even in this type of scenario. Therefore, if possible, it is recommended that you escort a student to the counseling center. This type of gesture of support can be reassuring for a student and will give you peace of mind knowing that the student did indeed go to the counseling center. If you are unable to do this yourself, you might try to arrange for someone else to escort the student as long as it is someone whom the student would be agreeable to.

The situation is more complicated when you are with a student that you believe should be seen immediately but the student refuses to go to the counseling office under any circumstances. Now you are faced with the dilemma of trying to get a student to do something against his or her wishes. This is an uncomfortable position to be in, but you can take measures to ensure that the student receives proper attention. Rather than try to convince an unwilling student to see a counselor, it is best to let the student leave and then contact either an administrative officer such as the dean of students or speak with one of the staff members in the counseling center. These individuals will take steps to ensure that an assessment is made and that the student is not at risk in any way. Generally speaking, it is somewhat easier to intervene in these kinds of situations with students who live on campus because numerous individuals in residence life are available to intercede.

Another troublesome scenario is having a sense of urgency about a student in your presence after regular office hours have ended. There is no need to panic in this type of situation because most campuses will have some type of emergency procedure in place. Although some counseling centers may keep evening hours, many are likely be closed during the evening. However, counseling centers typically have someone available for emergencies through an on-call system in which the person can be accessed anytime by being called or paged. Because it is vital to know about this procedure, I devote more attention to this in Chapter 7. For now, simply be aware that your campus should have some type of system in place for crisis or emergency situations and usually this is accessed through campus police or public safety. In addition, counseling centers usually give instructions for emergencies on their office voice mail for calls that come in after hours.

FOLLOWING UP

Follow-up is an essential part of the referral process. As a referral agent, you will likely feel reassured once a student has agreed to see a counselor. After making a referral that appears to be successful, you may be inclined to make certain assumptions. For example, you may assume that the student made and kept an appointment, has begun to receive help from a counselor, and that there is nothing more that you need to do. In the majority of cases, troubled students who you are able to persuade to see a counselor will indeed do so and may begin to experience some immediate improvement and alleviation of distress. However, this will not be the case for all students. Some students may never actually schedule an appointment, which is why it can be good sometimes to help the student do this at the time you make the referral. Of course, making an appointment does not guarantee that the student will keep the appointment. Some students have a habit of undermining any possibility of benefiting from counseling by not keeping scheduled appointments. It is also common for some students to enter counseling but discontinue after only one or two sessions. Consequently, you may assume that a student you referred is working with a counselor when this is not the case. This is why follow-up can be so important, especially with students who reluctantly agree to accept your referral.

Whenever possible, you should attempt to follow up directly with a student in a week or two after making the referral. This will usually involve a kind of "check in" to see how the student is doing and whether an initial appointment was made and kept. For students that tell you that they have not yet made an appointment, you can again encourage them to do so and offer to help arrange an appointment for them. Most students will be honest with you, but in some instances students may lie or mislead you into believing that they saw a counselor when they did not do so. More often, students may give the impression that they tried to make an appointment but could not get one.

Rather than be straightforward with you, perhaps because they fear negative consequences, some students will say just about anything to make it appear as if they were willing to seek counseling but ran into some type of problem. Students sometimes negatively distort their experience of going to the counseling center for an initial appointment as a way to justify not following through any further with counseling. Although there may be instances of counseling center problems with scheduling or other matters, which can indeed lessen a student's willingness to return, often these are minor errors or miscommunications that become exaggerated or blown out of proportion by students who are resistant or reluctant to seek counseling. This is particularly true for students who are persuaded by others to go for counseling.

Because of the potential for some students to mislead or distort in this way, it might be preferable to conduct some measure of follow-up with the counseling center as well as the student whenever you have reason to doubt what a student tells you and in cases in which the student grudgingly agrees to accept your referral. As discussed earlier, for you to be able to follow up with the counseling office, you need to have the student agree to this at the time you make the referral. Assuming you have done this, you can subsequently contact the counseling office to see if the student was seen.

If you call the counseling office and are told that verification of student contact cannot be released without student consent, then this means that the student either (a) neglected to discuss with the counselor your request for confirmation of attendance or (b) decided not to give consent for this. The latter situation would be extremely rare because students do not typically have any problem with referral sources getting confirmation of their initial appointment. In this scenario it is most likely that the student simply forgot to ask the counselor about giving permission to allow you to know that the appointment was kept. Your call to the counseling office, albeit unsuccessful in getting verification, will at least prompt the counselor to discuss this issue with the student if the student returns for a second appointment. If the student fails to give consent for release of confidential information, then your only recourse is to follow up directly with the student.

Restrictions of Confidentiality of Counseling

Confidentiality is perhaps the cornerstone of counseling. People need to feel reassured that what they share in counseling is kept in confidence unless they agree to have specific information released to others. College students who enter counseling value confidentiality and prefer that little information be revealed to others (VandeCreek, Miars, & Herzog, 1987). But confidentiality can seem like an obstacle for those who simply wish to follow up on students they refer. Others on campus who refer students often pressure college counselors to reveal confidential information (Gilbert, 1989; Malley, Gallagher, & Brown, 1992; Sharkin, 1995). A survey of common referral agents in a college community showed that a majority expected to have access to confidential information, and an even greater number believed they *should* have access (Sharkin, Scappaticci, & Birky, 1995). Referral agents can have negative reactions to restrictions of confidentiality about referred students (Birky, Sharkin, Marin & Scappaticci, 1998). As an example, Boswinkel (1987) expressed frustrations associated with confidentiality as a resident assistant who often referred fellow students to the counseling center.

Clearly, confidentiality can pose potential complications and dilemmas for referral agents who wish to follow up on students they refer. College counselors generally understand and respect the need for others on campus to be informed about the attendance and progress of the students they refer. College counselors do not intend to be uncooperative by withholding information but need to preserve confidentiality and cannot release any information without client consent. Without a student's permission, counselors cannot even confirm whether they had contact with a student. At times this may alienate or anger concerned others and strain relations with other members of the campus community (Sharkin, 1995).

Speaking from my own experience, I generally prefer when there is some type of communication with the referral source before I ever meet with a student. This allows me not only to obtain some background on why the person referred the student but also presents the opportunity to discuss with the referring person the issue of follow-up and need for student consent. It lets me know immediately whether the individual is concerned enough to want some sort of follow-up and how we will handle this.

It can be much more problematic when I receive an unexpected request for confirmation of contact with a student but do not have the student's permission to release this information. Sometimes this occurs during informal interactions such as while walking across campus. When this happens, I need to explain that I cannot release information without a student's consent but would be willing to try to obtain consent if I have contact with the student. I will also suggest to concerned others that they speak to students about their desire to follow up with the counseling office and explore whether students would be agreeable to this. This can be awkward when people assume that students are in counseling when in fact this is not so. It would be much easier if I could just be straightforward about attendance in counseling, but this would be unethical on my part and might actually lessen the likelihood of prospective students ever coming to see me. Students would not feel particularly safe about seeing a counselor who casually confirms counseling attendance (or nonattendance) with others on campus without their knowledge or consent.

Once you have verified that a referred student did go to the counseling center for at least an initial session, you should still continue to periodically follow up with the student if you remain concerned about how the student is doing. An initial session with a counselor at least ensures that the student is evaluated and offered ongoing counseling. Sometimes an initial session is enough to get a student "hooked in" and open to continued sessions. In addition, when a student keeps an initial session this means that a member of the counseling staff now has familiarity with that student. This can be helpful in the event you feel the need to contact the counseling office again with new or lingering concerns related to a particular student you had already referred once. Contact with the dean of students or senior administrative officer in student services is always a good option as well, particularly if the counseling office is unable to discuss a particular student's situation.

SUMMARY

Following some general guidelines can facilitate the referral of students to counseling. The referral process can be conceptualized as a "transfer of trust" whereby referral agents promote a sense of trust in the counseling office and make students active participants in the decision to seek help. It can be especially helpful to prepare students for what to expect when going to see a campus counselor and establish positive expectations for counseling. Therefore, it is important to have some knowledge of the counseling center staff, functions, and services available. For situations involving more urgency, additional steps may need to be taken to ensure that a student receives prompt attention. Follow-up represents an important part of the referral process, but potential complications can be associated with confidentiality of counseling. Problems can be minimized when counselors have an opportunity to communicate with referral agents before meeting with students referred for counseling.

Chapter 6

Specific Issues and Populations
to Consider

It should be apparent to the reader by now that recognizing and responding to students in distress can be quite challenging at times. The
purpose of this chapter is to examine and discuss some specific issues
that can either exacerbate efforts to help students or pose additional
challenges and complications. Some of these issues were briefly tou-
ched on earlier yet warrant further elaboration. The issues addressed
in this chapter are

1. how much responsibility to assume when trying to help students
   in distress;
2. awareness of potential dual-role and boundary complications;
3. dealing with parents of distressed students; and
4. dealing with peers of distressed students.

This chapter also devotes attention to issues that should be considered when assisting distressed students who are members of the following populations or groups:

1. students of color;
2. international students;
3. gay, lesbian, and bisexual students;
4. student-athletes; and
5. graduate students.

Each of these groups are discussed in terms of special considerations
that one might need to be sensitive to when trying to facilitate a referral to counseling.

College Students in Distress
© 2006 by The Haworth Press, Inc. All rights reserved.
doi:10.1300/5228_06

HOW MUCH RESPONSIBILITY TO ASSUME

My caveat for faculty and staff members to avoid assuming too much responsibility when responding to students in distress warrants further discussion. Granted, at times it can be difficult not to assume a lot of responsibility with students whom you like and have come to know well. Some students may even try to convince you that you are the best or only person that can truly help. However, taking on a lot of responsibility for students can ultimately lead to feelings of anger, frustration, and resentment, as well as cause considerable stress and anxiety for faculty and staff members. This is particularly likely to happen in situations that become increasingly troublesome and time-consuming.

Imagine for a moment that a student you are familiar with approaches you and asks if he can talk to you about a "personal problem." You agree and he proceeds to disclose concerns about how others perceive him. He speaks about being introverted and anxious in most social situations. There is nothing that unusual about what he shares and he seems open and comfortable with you. After a little while he tells you that it was helpful to talk to you and that it felt more comfortable with you than a counselor he had spoken to recently. The student then asks if he can meet with you again in another few days.

This might seem like a fairly innocuous scenario in which you could probably imagine being available to help the student. You may even feel somewhat compelled to try to help given that he told you how comfortable he felt talking to you. It might not even cross your mind to try to refer him to the counseling center after he said that he was more comfortable with you than a counselor. It is reasonable to expect that another meeting with the student will be similar to the first one. Thus, assume you agree to meet with the student again.

Now imagine that the second meeting is much different from the first. This time the student appears more distressed and speaks in a way that is somewhat vague and confusing at times. He tells you that he believes other students must perceive him as weird and suspects that others talk about him. He gives examples of others staring at him both in class and other public places and talking to one another about how strange he looks. As he is talking, you begin to feel uneasy and wonder about the seriousness of his problem. This arouses much more concern than when he had first spoken to you. You now decide that it might be best for him to speak to a counselor on campus and suggest this to him. He responds with anger, reminding you that he told you that he was not comfortable speaking to a counselor. He becomes defensive and seems offended by your suggestion. He states that you must think he is weird, just like everyone else, and then he leaves. You remain concerned yet are unsure of what to do next.

This hypothetical scenario is not intended to heighten your anxiety or make you fearful of helping a student in distress, but rather to illustrate how a situation that initially appears benign can subsequently become more troublesome. If the student had first presented as he did in the second meeting, most likely you would not have agreed to meet with him again and instead would have attempted to refer him back to the counseling office. Even though he might have been just as unlikely to agree to the referral, this would have established a clear boundary and avoided any expectation on his part that you could help him with personal problems. This scenario is actually not much different from what occurs in counseling. That is, some students initially present with concerns or problems that appear to be normal developmental struggles, but then more serious issues emerge in subsequent sessions.

You can be helpful and responsive to distressed students without putting yourself in the role of a surrogate counselor. It is my opinion that the prospect of getting involved in something bigger than what you first imagined makes it too risky to do more than serve as a referral agent. Moreover, you could inadvertently end up doing more harm than good because by being available to a student in a surrogate counselor capacity could lessen the student's inclination or willingness to get professional help if needed. I recommend that you maintain clear boundaries from the outset and simply help distressed students get proper care from the appropriate resources on campus.

AWARENESS OF DUAL-ROLE
AND BOUNDARY COMPLICATIONS

Dual-role and boundary issues can emerge in a number of ways on a college campus to further complicate matters when trying to respond to and refer troubled students to counseling. Many individuals who work on a college campus assume a variety of roles with students. For example, some faculty and staff members will serve as advisors to student clubs and organizations. Consequently, faculty and staff members may interact with and come to know students in multiple contexts.

Boundary issues can also occur as a result of students being employed or serving as volunteers in offices and departments on campus. It is common for students to work as office assistants, desk receptionists, teaching assistants, research assistants, and in other capacities across a campus. Students often do volunteer work as well. I was once the coordinator of a peer education program that consisted almost exclusively of student volunteers. In addition, students volunteer to serve as student representatives on university-wide and departmental committees alongside faculty and staff committee members. Also, a certain percentage of students on campus will be children or relatives of faculty and staff members, which can pose its own unique set of boundary issues when these students experience serious emotional problems.

Dual-role and boundary issues are well recognized within the field of college counseling (Harris, 2002; Iosupovici & Luke, 2002). Dual relationships are often unavoidable for the college counselor who typically assumes many roles on a campus. In addition to their primary function of counseling students, college counselors will often be actively involved in activities such as teaching, advising, supervising, and conducting outreach and programming. As a result, college counselors can sometimes find themselves in awkward and ethically dubious situations that might place strains on confidentiality (Sharkin, 1995).

I have had numerous situations involving dual-role issues arise over the years. As an example, I once worked in a counseling center where we hired work-study students to help with various tasks in the office. One time a female student employed in our office came in with one of her friends who she thought needed to see a counselor right away. I happened to be available to meet with the student in distress, but to my surprise she insisted that her friend (our work-study student) be present in the session. Despite some mild awkwardness, I agreed and proceeded with the session. My intent was to focus on the distressed student and simply considered the other student as being present for her moral support. However, after a little while the work-study student began to interject with some of her own distress in response to hearing her friend self-disclose in the session. The work-study student became quite upset and revealed serious problems, including having been the victim of childhood abuse. Naturally I had to respond to her as well, and thus I found myself counseling a student whom I still needed to do errands for me in the office.

I believe this is an important issue for two reasons. First, it might be helpful for members of a campus community to keep in mind that some students you attempt to refer to counseling may have preestablished noncounseling associations with certain counselors, which could potentially complicate the referral process. Whenever possible, alternative arrangements and appropriate outside referrals will be made for students who might not be able to see counselors on campus due to these dual-role complications. For example, the work-study student in the example was subsequently assigned to a counselor trainee who did not need the student to do any office-related errands.

Second, at some point you may find yourself needing to respond to a student in distress who has a close association with you or your department. It might be a student who works in your office or department, serves on a committee with you, or is a member of a student group that you advise. This does not necessarily mean that you need to do anything different in terms of responding and making a referral, but it can be awkward to have to deal with students in this way and then resume your other role with them. It can be helpful sometimes to discuss this issue with students in order to alleviate anxiety or awkwardness about it. Supervisors of student employees who experience severe psychological distress might have concerns about how the student's work will be affected. This too should be openly discussed at the proper time with the student but does require a delicate balance between sensitivity to the student's situation and the responsibilities as the student's supervisor.

DEALING WITH PARENTS
OF DISTRESSED STUDENTS

Issues related to dealing with parents of distressed students could probably comprise an entire resource guide all their own. Whereas resource guides have been written for parents of college students (Barkin, 1999; Coburn & Treeger, 1997; Johnson & Schelhas-Miller,

2000), there is no resource guide for college personnel on how to deal with parents. When parents are concerned about their children's emotional well-being while at college, they will call whomever they believe can assist. Aside from the counseling or student health office, this might be faculty advisors, residential life staff, public safety officers, and deans. Some parents might feel that their child's situation warrants the attention of a top-level administrator or even the university president. It is not unusual for parents to call the school in an effort to get their child into counseling, and they may try to enlist the help of various individuals on campus to make this happen. Although some parents will be able to directly refer their children to campus counseling, others will not necessarily have such easy influence, especially if there is significant conflict in their relationships with their children. However, unless it is a crisis or emergency, parents need to know that their children cannot be forced into counseling.

In addition to responding to concerned parents, there may be times when college personnel need to contact parents because their children are experiencing significant distress while at school. College personnel typically first obtain student consent for parental contact, though contact might occur without consent in an emergency situation. The process of contacting parents about distressed students can arouse anxiety for college personnel because of the nature of the situation and uncertainty about how parents will respond.

Based on my experiences of dealing with parents of distressed students, I find that parents tend to fall into two divergent camps. On the one side are parents who show support and willingness to do whatever they can to help without being overbearing or unreasonable. These are the parents who call the school when concerned about their child to see who is in the best position to help and will be appropriately concerned and responsive when someone at the school needs to contact them. These parents will be reasonable in terms of what they expect the school to do for their child and will be available to assist however they can (e.g., allowing the student to return home temporarily if necessary).

On the other side are parents who come across as overly demanding, unreasonable, and unpleasant to deal with on an interpersonal level. They may display a sense of entitlement because they pay the tuition bills and expect the school to take care of everything without much involvement on their part. These parents may even seem annoyed or defensive when informed about their troubled child, as if their child's problems at school cause a disruption in their own lives. These parents will be strongly resistant to the idea of having the student return home unless absolutely necessary.

Often the parents who respond in a negative manner are individuals who have their own significant personal problems. When I speak to parents about their troubled children they sometimes reveal some of their own distress such as financial or health problems. Not surprisingly, you often discover that parents of a troubled student have a long history of problems with the child and perhaps with other children in the family as well. Thus, it is understandable that some parents will react in a negative or antagonistic way when their child has emotional difficulties at college because of the additional stress it brings, especially if there have been problems like this in the past. It is also important to remember that parents will often feel quite powerless to do anything, particularly if they live a long distance from the school, and powerlessness can transform into anger and frustration.

Trying to be empathic even with overtly hostile or difficult parents can help diffuse the situation or at least lessen your own level of anger or anxiety. Being argumentative or defensive with parents will make the situation only more troublesome and stressful. It can be helpful to try to view parents as allies rather than adversaries regardless of how you experience them. As much as possible we need to avoid alienating parents because they have the potential to provide important information and serve as a valuable asset when trying to get proper care for troubled students (Sharkin, 1995). Sometimes parents of troubled students respond well when you acknowledge and help manage their anxiety about the situation by reassuring them that the school is doing or will do what it can to ensure their child's well-being. Although some parents will remain difficult or angry no matter what you say or do, the majority of parents do seem to come through in the end when they realize that their child's well-being is at stake.

Similar to my caveat about not assuming too much responsibility for troubled students, the same principle applies when dealing with their parents. Whenever a parent contacts you and expresses concerns about a student's emotional or psychological well-being, encourage the parent to consult with someone in the campus counseling center. College counselors are well accustomed to addressing such concerns from parents and can make recommendations or refer the parents to other resources if appropriate. Likewise, whenever there is consideration of contacting parents of a distressed student, it might be wise to seek the assistance and support of the counseling office if not already involved in the matter.

DEALING WITH PEERS OF DISTRESSED STUDENTS

Students often try to help their friends, roommates, and romantic partners with emotional problems such as depression (Sharkin, Plageman, & Mangold, 2003). In their efforts to help their troubled peers, students may turn to faculty and staff members for advice on what to do. Such situations can often be handled by simply referring concerned students to the counseling office. Indeed, it was found that students with concerns about other students might not be aware that they can contact the campus counseling service to consult about fellow students (Sharkin et al., 2003). However, some students might simply choose not to consult with a counselor because they fear that by doing so will prompt some type of action and perhaps get their peers in trouble at the school.

Like faculty and staff members, students can fall into the same trap of assuming too much responsibility when it comes to helping students in distress. I have had many consultations with students who presented with concerns about their peers and it has been quite eye-opening for me to see the lengths that some students will go to help their troubled peers. These students usually relent and contact the counseling center once they realize they are in over their heads. They may get scared about the level of distress of a fellow student or get to a point where their efforts are consuming too much time and energy without having much effect. Students trying to help troubled peers can themselves become significantly distressed and experience a disruption in their academic and social functioning as a result of their peer-helping efforts.

Whenever a student who has concerns about another student approaches you, it is generally best to try to convince the student to consult with a campus counselor. You can reassure the student that the consultation can remain anonymous and no names need to be given. The one exception to this is when there are concerns about a student being at risk for harm to self or others; counselors would certainly try to obtain the name of a student identified as at risk but could not force the concerned student to reveal it. For nonurgent concerns, students should be told that they can have the option of consulting with a counselor either by phone or in person regarding how to handle the situation and how to facilitate a referral to counseling.

The one thing that you do not want to do is collude with students in terms of avoiding getting troubled peers proper care when needed. Granted, students can exaggerate or misperceive the severity of peer troubles, but risks are associated with obtaining information about a troubled student and not responding adequately. You should make every effort to see that an administrative official or counselor has an opportunity to at least evaluate the specific situation. I usually try to talk to students who are concerned about a peer about the potential costs of caring and how caring sometimes means taking steps to enlist help from the proper resources. It can also be reassuring to tell students that even though the troubled peer might initially be upset or angry, he or she will ultimately realize that reaching out to others to get help for the peer came out of genuine concern and caring.

STUDENTS OF COLOR

In addition to common forms of distress experienced while in college, students of color can also experience distress specifically associated with culture and race such as discrimination, racism, racial identity development, and language and cultural barriers (Brinson & Kottler, 1995b; Constantine, Wilton, & Caldwell, 2003; Nishimura, 1998; Walden, 1994). Students of color include but are not limited to African American, Hispanic and Latino American, Asian American, and Native American students. The special issues and needs of biracial and multiracial students should not be overlooked as well (Nishimura, 1998). In contrast with their white peers, students of color can experience unique forms of distress within the context of their academic and social life on campus, such as instructor or classroom biases, subtle forms of stereotyping and racism, erroneous attributions or assumptions made on the basis of race, negative reactions to interracial dating, and other behaviors that cause strained race relations or create a hostile campus climate. In addition, students of color in a predominantly white institution are susceptible to social alienation and isolation (Brinson & Kottler, 1995b).

Despite these unique struggles, students of color are much less inclined to utilize counseling than white students (Brinson & Kottler, 1995b; Constantine, Chen, & Ceesay, 1997; Leong, Wagner, & Tata, 1995; Narikiyo & Kameoka, 1992; Walden, 1994). The underutilization of counseling by students of color has been attributed to factors such as shame or stigma associated with counseling (Constantine et al., 1997; Narikiyo & Kameoka, 1992), the absence of ethnically similar counseling professionals (Brinson & Kottler, 1995; Constantine et al., 1997), and mistrust or perceptions of campus counselors as insensitive to racial and cultural differences (Brinson & Kottler, 1995b; Leong et al., 1995; Nickerson, Helms, & Terrell, 1994). Students' level of racial identity development can also influence their willingness to seek counseling (Nickerson et al., 1994).

When personal problems are experienced, many students of color will seek help from sources not directly linked with counseling centers (Constantine et al., 1997). This might include academic advisors, financial aid officers, and staff members devoted to diversity and multicultural affairs on campus. Other sources of social support such as family members, peers, and involvement in religious or spiritual activity can also serve to lessen the need for professional counseling assistance (Constantine et al., 2003). When students of color do seek counseling on campus, they are more likely than white students to discontinue prematurely (Brinson & Kottler, 1995b). One possible reason for this may be incongruence between students' expectations of counseling and the actual counseling experience.

In an examination of a sample of case files of students of color who sought counseling on campus over the course of an academic year, Constantine et al. (1997) found that relationship difficulties with family members and depression were common presenting concerns. For students of color that have a particularly strong family orientation, they might experience a significant amount of distress when problems emerge within the family or with specific family members. It is possible that depression sometimes results from such family-related distress, though this was not specifically explored in the study. It must be kept in mind, however, that the findings may not be representative of students of color at other schools or even of all students of color at the school where the study was conducted, given the high percentage of students of color who do not seek counseling. The identified presenting concerns may simply be a reflection of a relatively small sample of students who were willing to seek counseling. Moreover, students of color may sometimes seek help for problems other than what is truly causing them the most distress; for example, Asian American students often present with academic concerns when they experience emotional distress (Cheng, Leong, & Geist, 1993).

Depending on your role on campus, you may be approached by or approach students of color who are experiencing emotional distress. In light of the challenges of referring students of color to counseling, such students may be more receptive if they can be referred to ethnically or racially similar counselors. However, simple matching of students and counselors on the basis of race (and other demographics) does not guarantee good matches. As an example, a student and counselor of the same race who are at different stages in their racial identity development might experience friction and not work well together. I usually recommend asking students if they have a preference regarding seeing a counselor similar in race or ethnic background. Some students will consider counseling only if they have the option of seeing a counselor of similar race, whereas for others counselor race has no bearing on whether they pursue counseling.

Counseling centers have made strong recruitment and retention efforts in order to diversify staff composition over the past several years, but an absence of counselors of color is still a reality at many institutions. In addition to the efforts to increase diversity in the field of college counseling, there have also been significant efforts over the years to devote more attention to multicultural issues in the training of counselors. Thus, increasing numbers of college counselors are being trained to be sensitive and responsive to the experiences and needs of students of color. In my own experience, I have found that visibility and direct involvement with students of color in noncounseling activities and events enhances the likelihood that they will come to see me for counseling. I believe that more and more college counselors realize this and work to proactively reach out to students of color.

For students of color who are having problems but seem unlikely to accept a referral to counseling, one option is to utilize others on campus who might be able to provide support and perhaps serve as a more influential conduit to the counseling center. When looking for assistance with personal problems, some students of color may feel more comfortable with a less formal or structured setting than a counseling office. Such a setting could be a multicultural student center or lounge that is commonly used by students of color. Faculty and staff members (including counselors) who serve as advisors to specific student groups or affiliates of a multicultural center may be willing to meet with students in these informal settings. In addition, most campuses should have an office of multicultural affairs or individuals designated to help meet the special needs of students of color, representing another possible resource for assisting students of color with personal problems.

INTERNATIONAL STUDENTS

International students represent another population of students that face unique sources of stress such as culture shock, language barriers, social isolation, and changes in social and economic status (Clark Oropeza, Fitzgibbon, & Baron, 1991; Lin, 2000; Mori, 2000; Pedersen, 1991). In addition, international students may be a population that is at increased risk for suicide (Schwartz & Whitaker, 1990). Thus, although many international students could benefit from using counseling services on campus, they generally tend not to use such services (Bradley, Parr, Lan, Bingi, & Gould, 1995; Brinson & Kottler, 1995a; Lin, 2000; Martinez, Huang, Johnson, & Edwards, 1989; Mori, 2000; Pedersen, 1991). International students who do seek counseling tend to discontinue prematurely compared to American students (Pedersen, 1991).

The underutilization of counseling services by international students has been attributed to several factors. It may be considered improper in certain cultures to discuss personal matters with strangers, so if it becomes necessary to seek help from others some international students prefer to go to people they know or are familiar with (Hayes & Lin, 1994; Martinez et al., 1989). Many international students (particularly from non-Western countries) are unfamiliar with or have misconceptions of counseling (Mori, 2000) or will not see counseling services as the place to get help (Martinez et al., 1989). They may instead seek help from an academic advisor or seek medical treatment when they experience personal problems. Some students may have concerns about American counselors not understanding the traditions, values, and other aspects of their native culture (Mori, 2000). Fears may even be associated with being sent home as failures if they were to seek professional counseling help on campus (Boyer & Sedlacek, 1989).

Because of their reluctance to seek counseling, international students are likely to avoid seeking help until a crisis occurs, and even then to seek help when compelled by others to do so (Martinez et al., 1989). When in crisis, international students may come across as quite demanding due to extreme stress and a desire for fast relief (Lin, 2000). Clark Oropeza et al. (1991) identified some of the unique circumstances and challenges involved in trying to manage mental health crises experienced by international students. They noted, for instance, that it could be difficult to recognize and diagnose serious psychological problems in the international student population because of the potential influence of cultural factors. There can also be complications associated with confidentiality when there is a need to interrupt or reduce a student's course of study due to mental health problems. Such complications may arise from Citizenship and Immigration Service regulations, financial sponsorship by a foreign government or agency, and language barriers. In extreme cases, difficult questions might emerge such as whether a student should be sent home, and if so, what types of mental health services are available in the student's home country and how this might affect the possibility of reentry.

Given that international students are likely to seek help from people they are familiar with, they are more inclined to approach faculty and staff members they know rather than counselors when they experience distress. The reluctance of many international students to use counseling will make the process of referral much more challenging and in some cases nearly impossible. The chances for a successful referral could be enhanced if there is someone on the counseling staff who has an international background (particularly if similar to the student's culture) or a special interest in working with international students.

Responding to an international student in distress may require that other resources be explored, at least initially. For example, it might be important to seek assistance from or refer students to people on campus who work closely with the international student population (Mori, 2000) such as those in the offices of international studies and English as a second language. Also, it can sometimes be helpful to enlist assistance from faculty and staff members who are from or have a keen understanding of a particular student's home country to serve as consultants or interpreters. These other resources might be in a better position to then make the referral to the counseling office if necessary.

GAY, LESBIAN, AND BISEXUAL STUDENTS

Students who self-identify as gay, lesbian, and bisexual (GLB) may be particularly vulnerable to serious mental health problems such as depression that largely result from difficulties with developing a sexual orientation identity (D'Augelli, 1993). Although little research has been conducted regarding transgender college students, we may assume that they face similar risks. GLB students typically progress through stages of identity development (Meyer & Schwitzer, 1999), but the process can be complicated by a lack of support and oppressive forces within the larger culture (Palma & Stanley, 2002). GLB students must contend with heterosexism, homophobia, negative and hostile attitudes, harassment, and violence that are often directed toward them on campus (D'Augelli, 1992, 1993; D'Augelli & Rose, 1990). In addition to discrimination and victimization experiences, GLB students may struggle with their own sense of anxiety, guilt, shame, and religious conflicts associated with being a sexual minority. The results of one study (Westefeld, Maples, Buford, & Taylor, 2001) suggest that GLB students may be particularly vulnerable to depression, loneliness, and suicide risk.

Many GLB students have clarity about their sexual orientation dating back to earlier precollege years, whereas others may first experience such clarity during their college years. Some students go through a process of "questioning" before experiencing a sense of clarity and coming to terms with being GLB. Regardless of when they first become aware of their orientation, GLB individuals need to decide whether to "come out," and if so, to whom. Some students may question their orientation based on sexual fantasies and desires with members of the same sex, but such feelings may or may not equate with sexual orientation. Green (1998) has described how students may experience pressure to prematurely declare a sexual orientation identity that might be inconsistent with their sense of self. According to Green, this may stem from the individual's inability to tolerate uncertainty and/or society's intolerance of ambiguity. Such pressures can cause confusion and emotional distress for students who are going through a period of questioning.

The GLB student community on most campuses will consist of both students who are out and those who feel the need to conceal their sexual orientation from others and perhaps even the need to posture as heterosexual. The latter students may fear the consequences of coming out or of being "outed" against their wishes. The specific climate of a school has the potential to increase or lessen such fears. Simply stated, some campuses will be much more open and supportive of GLB students than others. For example, there may be a strong and visible GLB student group or organization on some campuses but not on others.

When responding to GLB students in distress, particularly when the distress appears to be associated with being GLB, it can be helpful to assist these students in finding a caring and supportive community within the larger campus community. This could be in the form of a counseling support group (Welch, 1996) or a campus GLB student group. GLB students are likely to be receptive to counseling as long as they perceive their campus counseling center as a safe and accepting environment with staff members who are sensitive to their unique struggles. Because some GLB students will have a preference for a GLB counselor (McDermott, Tyndall, & Lichtenberg, 1989), it is helpful for campus faculty and staff to know if any counseling center staff members self-identify as GLB. If no GLB counselors are available, then the next best option is to refer to a counselor who is likely to be sensitive to GLB issues. For example, many counselors become involved in GLB groups and events regardless of their sexual orientation.

The same principles hold true when trying to get assistance for students that give any indication that they are going through a period of questioning or other struggle with sexual identity. They are likely to be receptive to meeting with a counselor in a safe and confidential environment and may respond well to a recommendation to see someone identified as sensitive to and able to help students with such struggles.

STUDENT-ATHLETES

College student-athletes are considered another unique population of students that have distinctive needs and are at risk for particular forms of psychological distress (Parham, 1993; Pinkerton, Hinz, & Barrow, 1989). Compared to nonathletes, student-athletes face additional challenges and pressures associated with their athletic involvement such as balancing athletic and academic demands, managing anxiety related to competition and performance, managing athletic success and failure, maintaining optimal physical conditioning, and being socially isolated from mainstream campus activity (Parham, 1993; Pinkerton et al., 1989). These students may be particularly vulnerable to eating disorders (Johnson, Powers, & Dick, 1999; Seime & Damer, 1991) as well as anxiety, depression, and substance abuse (Damm & Murray, 1996; Hinkle, 1996; Miller, Miller, Verhegge, Linville, & Pumariega, 2002). The psychological impact of an injury or other circumstance that limits or precludes athletic participation can be particularly devastating for students whose identity revolves strongly around athletics. For example, an injured athlete might experience a sense of identity loss that in turn can result in depression and despair.

There may be some key differences in student-athletes as a function of gender. Female student-athletes have been found to be especially prone to issues with weight, body image, and eating-disordered behavior (Cogan & Petrie, 1996). Female athletes might also experience distress in response to negative attitudes and stereotypes about female participation in sports, especially in more male-oriented sports such as basketball and lacrosse (Cogan & Petrie, 1996).

Student-athletes have been identified as yet another group of students that are not inclined to use counseling (Pinkerton et al., 1989). There may be various reasons for their underutilization of counseling. For example, student-athletes have been characterized as possessing a general tendency to deny emotional problems (Pinkerton et al., 1989). According to Pinkerton et al. this form of denial may be associated with the athlete's self-image as independent and self-reliant and not wanting to appear vulnerable or weak. Another possible reason that student-athletes underutilize counseling is that they tend to receive strong social support from their involvement in sports programs. Conversely, the loss of such support, for instance due to injury or conflict with coaches or teammates, could trigger severe emotional distress.

Student-athletes will sometimes seek counseling in order to appease or comply with a coach or athletic trainer who urges them to do so. For better or worse, coaches and trainers have the coercive power to mandate student-athletes to counseling. For college personnel other than coaches and trainers, the ability to make a referral may be more challenging. Referring students can be made somewhat easier if some counselors on campus have special interest or skills in working with athletes. Sports psychology has been a growing field over the past several years and is increasingly recognized as an important specialty in college counseling. Some college counselors might even serve as consultants to specific athletic teams, enabling easier referrals to counseling when necessary. If no counselors on campus are identified as working closely with athletes, it is possible that practitioners in the nearby community will identify sport psychology as a specialty.

Without the possibility of making a referral to a specific counselor who has worked with student-athletes, the best that one can do is to make a convincing case for seeing a counselor that counteracts the typical reservations that student-athletes might have. For example, counseling could be characterized as a way to actively sort through and resolve problems with the aid of an objective listener as opposed to it being a passive form of receiving help from someone else. It can also be helpful to characterize seeking counseling as a sign of strength rather than weakness. The issue of confidentiality might need to be reinforced with student-athletes, for they may have fears that certain problems such as substance abuse or eating-disordered behavior might be revealed to coaches or others.

GRADUATE STUDENTS

Graduate students represent another population of students that can pose unique challenges when they experience emotional distress. Unfortunately, graduate students per se have not received the same kind of attention in the literature as the student populations discussed earlier. Some research shows that graduate students in their first and second year of graduate study experience high levels of stress, anxiety, and depression (Goplerud, 1980; Hodgson & Simoni, 1995). In addition, students age twenty-five and older, representing graduate students and nontraditionally aged undergraduates, have been found to have higher rates of suicide than younger students (Silverman et al., 1997). In contrast with traditionally aged undergraduates, graduate students tend to be more diverse in age and life experience and can be burdened with different financial, familial, and academic responsibilities. In an examination of a large sample of first- and second-year doctoral students, Hodgson and Simoni (1995) found that the students who reported greater psychological distress were less satisfied with graduate school, had less perceived academic success, less social support, and more financial problems.

The demands of graduate study can contribute to unique forms of distress and in some cases may precipitate an emotional crisis. For example, students might become highly distressed in response to difficulty with meeting critical deadlines set forth by their graduate program, qualifying for or failing comprehensive exams, making progress on a thesis or dissertation, or obtaining or maintaining financial aid or an assistantship. The degree of support from faculty, especially one's advisor, can play a key role in the level of stress and distress experienced by graduate students (Goplerud, 1980; Hodgson & Simoni, 1995). Campus life for graduate students can also pose problems because they tend not to be as integrated socially on a campus. This can lead to feelings of social isolation, particularly for students who have no spouse or partner. Social isolation can be further intensified for international and ethnic minority graduate students. Significant struggles can also arise for students who try to complete their studies while working full-time and/or tending to family responsibilities (which is true for nontraditionally aged undergraduate students as well).

Graduate students have not been identified as a group that underutilizes counseling, and they may actually overutilize counseling compared to undergraduates on some campuses. Nevertheless, situational factors might hinder graduate students from being able to take advantage of counseling services on campus. Work and other responsibilities may make it difficult for these students to find the time for weekly counseling or to schedule appointments during the counseling center's regular office hours. Some graduate students might also be in need of services that are either not available on campus or that are more challenging to arrange, such as couples or family counseling. Graduate students in counseling or clinical psychology programs may not want to use counseling on campus because of dual-role complications (e.g., when they are receiving or expect to receive training and supervision in the counseling center).

When dealing with a graduate student in distress, many of the same principles that apply to undergraduates are appropriate. However, if certain circumstances emerge that lessen the student's ability or willingness to seek counseling on campus, it might still be helpful to encourage consultation (perhaps by phone) with the counseling office. For instance, if a student has concerns about using the services on campus or cannot keep weekday appointments, the counseling service could assist the student in obtaining affordable services within the community. Some counseling centers may even offer services specifically for graduate students such as a counseling or support group or evening hours that might make it easier for some students to make appointments.

SUMMARY

The process of responding to students in distress and referring them to counseling can pose an assortment of challenges. Specific issues that often need to be considered when dealing with students in distress include deciding upon the level of responsibility to assume for helping students, maintaining appropriate boundaries, managing potential complications regarding serving in multiple roles with students, and responding to parents, peers, and concerned others regarding students. In addition, students who are members of specific populations such as students of color and student-athletes can pose unique issues and challenges when they experience psychological distress. Being educated about the counseling service offerings and knowing counseling staff ethnicity and specialty areas can be especially useful in facilitating counseling referrals with these students.

Chapter 7

Campus Policies and Procedures Related to Student Mental Health

A number of policies and procedures associated with student mental health are common on college campuses. These policies cover a range of issues, such as accommodations for students with psychological disabilities, psychological emergencies, withdrawal and readmission, and mandatory counseling. The direct relevance of these policies will vary among college personnel depending on their role with students. However, it may be helpful for anyone who works with college students to be familiar with policies related to student mental health, particularly now that mental health issues appear to have a greater impact on campus life than ever before.

This chapter provides a review of the most common policies and guidelines related to student mental health. This material is divided into five sections. The process of evaluating and providing accommodations for students with psychological disabilities is discussed in the first section. The second section offers a discussion of procedures for handling psychological crises and emergencies. This is followed by a review of policies related to withdrawal from school and conditions for readmission. In the fourth section, the practice of mandatory counseling is addressed. The chapter closes with a brief discussion of limitations within the scope of counseling services that can be ethically and responsibly provided on campus.

ACCOMMODATIONS FOR STUDENTS WITH PSYCHOLOGICAL DISABILITIES

The Americans with Disabilities Act of 1990 extends legal protection from discrimination to individuals with emotional or psychological

College Students in Distress
© 2006 by The Haworth Press, Inc. All rights reserved.
doi:10.1300/5228_07

disorders (Rothstein, 1996). Examples of disabling conditions that would qualify under the law include anxiety and mood disorders, eating disorders, psychotic disorders, and recovery from substance abuse. The Office for Civil Rights is responsible for investigating cases and ensuring compliance with the guidelines stipulated by law.

Over the past several years, increasing attention has been devoted to compliance with the ADA guidelines for college students with psychological disabilities (Gibson, 2000; Unger, 1998). Most colleges are now required to have specific individuals or departments devoted exclusively to assisting students with physical, learning, and psychological disabilities, although collaboration among several departments or services will often be required (Jacobs & Glater, 1993).

Students with psychological disabilities may experience significant struggles within the academic environment. Based on a qualitative study of the college experiences of students with psychological disabilities, Megivern, Pellerito, and Mowbray (2003) identified a number of barriers these students experience, such as impairment in concentration, memory, and motivation, and difficulties integrating socially into campus life. Interestingly, they found that over 90 percent of their sample did not seek assistance from the campus counseling center or disability service. Megivern et al. theorized that many students might be reluctant to use these campus services because of fears of being dismissed from school due to their psychological problems. There might also be concern about negative attitudes and perceptions among faculty and staff that students with psychological disabilities are disruptive, incompetent, or dangerous (Unger, 1998; Wahl, 1999).

The process of providing accommodations under the ADA generally consists of three steps. First, the student must be evaluated by a qualified individual such as a licensed psychologist or psychiatrist who can provide a diagnosis and assessment of the severity of the disabling condition. The evaluator needs to describe how the disabling condition affects the student in the academic setting and make recommendations for need-based accommodations. Some students enter college already having completed this process and will therefore provide this documentation when they first arrive on campus. Ultimately, students bear the responsibility of providing proper documentation of the need for special accommodations.

Provided that valid documentation is submitted, the second step is to arrange for appropriate accommodations for the student. The accommodations need to be "reasonable" and need based. Accommodations or modifications can be refused if they fundamentally alter the nature of the academic program. As an example, if a student requests to have all exams as take-home tests because of a psychological condition such as panic disorder, this would likely be denied on the grounds that it fundamentally alters the university's program. Classroom accommodations that are commonly provided include alternate testing arrangements, tape recording of lectures, use of note-takers, tutoring, and certain exceptions to regular class attendance (e.g., being excused from class at certain times). Letters are typically sent to instructors to notify them of specific students who qualify for accommodations. In addition to in-class accommodations, some students might be permitted to carry a reduced course load. Students can also qualify for special accommodations in residential life. For example, a student diagnosed with Asperger's syndrome, an autistic-related condition involving severe social skill deficits, might be given a single room upon request.

The third step in the process consists of follow-up with the appropriate personnel on campus, typically the disability services office and/or the counseling office. Students with psychological disabilities might benefit from maintaining a relationship with the counseling office, but this should not be a condition of receiving special accommodations.

The number of students who qualify for accommodations due to psychiatric disabilities appears to be on the rise. However, a national survey of campus disability services suggests that many of these services may be ill-prepared or lack the resources needed to assist students with psychiatric disabilities (Collins & Mowbray, 2005). The survey also found that disability services vary considerably from campus to campus. Collins and Mowbray make several recommendations to bolster disability services on campuses, such as creating more training opportunities for disability services staff, faculty, and students.

PSYCHOLOGICAL CRISES AND EMERGENCIES

Psychological emergencies can emerge in many different ways on a campus, for example, when students are suicidal or suspected of being suicidal, experience the sudden death of family members or friends, are victims of sexual or nonsexual assaults, have unwanted pregnancies, or have panic attacks or psychotic episodes. A protocol should be in place on campus for responding to such an emergency, particularly when it occurs after regular working hours.

Missed Classes Due to Emotional Distress

There are times when students miss or need to miss class because of severe emotional distress. This may be a one-time occurrence or a more protracted situation across an entire semester. Sometimes students in distress miss class because they seek assistance in the counseling office at a time when they would ordinarily be in class. When a student misses class in order to see a counselor, simple confirmation of this from the counseling office (with the student's consent) is usually sufficient for the instructor. When a student seeks help after already missing class, this will require the counselor to make a determination of the legitimacy of the student's reason for being absent. When students inform their professors that they missed class due to emotional problems, professors may ask students to obtain a note from a counselor that validates that their absence from class was due to emotional distress.

The situation can be somewhat more challenging when students miss exams or other course requirements such as a lab or presentation or are unable to turn in an assignment on time because of emotional distress. It can be difficult sometimes for counselors to make an assessment of how much the student's emotional distress is a valid reason for missing an exam or failing to complete an assignment. As counselors, we do the best we can to assess each individual student's situation and inform instructors when we believe that a student's circumstance appears to warrant consideration of an opportunity to make up a missed exam or other work.

The degree of disruption from emotional distress can sometimes involve a more general impairment in academic functioning. For example, a student who is depressed over the loss of a relationship may struggle all semester to stay focused on academics and complete assignments on time. Students should speak directly with their professors when they experience such difficulties, but many are uncomfortable doing so. When students seek counseling help, this at least allows for the possibility that a counselor can serve as an advocate and help communicate with professors on students' behalf. If it is determined that a student's emotional or psychological difficulties are resulting in impaired academic functioning, then all options will be explored, including withdrawing or taking a grade of incomplete in one or more classes or temporarily withdrawing from school if necessary. However, emotionally impaired students are sometimes capable of completing their courses, particularly when professors are willing to provide opportunities for make-up work and other ways to aid such students.

With student consent, campus counselors will communicate directly with professors of students who are trying to complete their academic work under emotionally challenging circumstances, often by sending a letter through campus mail. An example of such a letter appears below.

> Dear Professor:
>   Stu Dent, who is enrolled in your Psychology 101 course, is currently experiencing emotional difficulties and is being seen in the office of Counseling Services. His ability to attend to his studies is certainly affected by his current difficulties. Please take this into consideration when Stu speaks to you regarding the possibility of making up work missed in your class. If the nature of the course and/or amount of work precludes him from being able to complete your course successfully, please discuss this with him so that he may consider the option of withdrawal. Stu will speak with you directly regarding making up missed work. If you have any questions regarding this matter, please contact me.

How professors use this information or handle such matters is at their discretion. In my experience, the majority of professors tend to be flexible and willing to do whatever they can within reason to help troubled students complete their courses.

After-Hours Crises

The protocol for responding to an emergency during regular operating hours is generally straightforward. Students in crisis will either refer themselves to the counseling office or be referred by another individual or office. Campus counselors should always be available to see students on a walk-in or emergency basis during normal operating hours. Emergencies that occur after hours, however, require additional resources to be in place. The majority of counseling centers provide after-hours or on-call services, which consist of round-the-clock crisis management coverage (Coulter, Offutt, & Mascher, 2003; Meilman, Hacker, & Kraus-Zeilmann, 1993). An on-call counselor is usually accessed through an emergency phone number, which is likely to be the number for campus police or public safety. This is one of the more important components of college counseling services, but its effectiveness depends on the collaborative efforts of various people and offices on campus, such as residential life, dean of students, and public safety.

An example of an actual emergency call will show how such a situation can emerge and unfold. This particular situation occurred at about 1:00 a.m. and involved a female student who made suicidal-like comments to her roommate just after her boyfriend broke up with her. Naturally the roommate became alarmed and decided to tell the resident assistant on the floor. The resident assistant then contacted the building director who in turn called public safety. An officer was dispatched to the residence to initially speak to the student and the officer decided to call the counselor-on-call (which happened to be me) to evaluate the student.

After being briefed by both the officer and roommate on what had occurred, I then spoke to the distressed student. She was upset but denied any intent to kill herself. She said she could understand how her comments to her roommate could be interpreted as suicidal threats, but she was adamant that she was not suicidal and denied making any suicide attempts in the past. I decided that it would be okay for her to remain in her room for the night and told her that I would follow up with her later in the day to see how she was doing. This was also used as an opportunity to encourage her to use counseling to help her deal with the breakup. I informed the officer that she was not suicidal and documented what had transpired.

Many of the after-hours crisis calls are like the one in this example. There is a concern for a student and a perceived need for immediate attention. Often it is determined that there is no imminent risk and an intervention by telephone is sufficient. However, there are occasions when the situation is much more serious and requires further action. If the student had admitted having suicidal intentions, then arrangements would have been made to further evaluate her on site and possibly initiate hospitalization. On some campuses, the protocol may involve having public safety transport students to a nearby hospital for further evaluation.

Residential life personnel may sometimes prefer to err on the side of caution and send a student home following an emergency incident, particularly if there is any concern of deliberate or accidental self-harm. This is understandable given the potential problems of having people with limited or no mental health background trying to monitor troubled students. Unlike college counselors, residential life staff members are not bound by the same restrictions of confidentiality and have more freedom to contact parents during emergencies even without student consent. In another after-hours incident, two room-mates were discovered to have been drinking and engaging in self-cutting. Although neither student was deemed to be suicidal, residential life staff remained concerned about their safety, especially given that they were both under the influence of alcohol. Thus, they decided to call the parents of both students to arrange for them to be escorted home at least for that night.

In general, after-hours situations that transpire on versus off campus are somewhat easier to manage. As the first example demonstrates, the on-call system can involve multiple individuals and a chain of command. The residential life component on most campuses will usually have a strong support system in place that increases the probability of a prompt response to a crisis situation. In contrast, students who do not reside on campus will not necessarily have the same type of readily available or accessible resources during a crisis situation. Another factor that can play a role in how well schools can handle after-hours emergencies is the size of the school. Larger schools may have the added benefit of greater availability of auxiliary services both on and off campus (Coulter et al., 2003). Conversely, smaller schools may be better able to detect and respond to student emergencies by virtue of having a more manageable number of students in the total student body.

Student Hospitalization

As alluded to in the previous section, arrangements sometimes need to be made to have students hospitalized, particularly when they are assessed to be at imminent risk of harm to themselves or others or when they experience psychotic episodes. Important considerations are involved in pursuing hospitalization, such as determining if an individual is willing to be hospitalized voluntarily or if involuntary commitment procedures need to be initiated (Ponterotto, 1987). Ideally, students deemed high risk would agree to voluntary hospitalization, which is often the case. Some students initiate hospitalization themselves either by presenting at an emergency room of their own accord or asking someone such as a friend to escort them to an emergency room.

When a student is taken to a hospital emergency room, this does not necessarily mean that he or she will be admitted. An evaluation will be made to determine if inpatient care is necessary. If inpatient treatment is not deemed necessary, the student may be allowed to leave, with or without alternative outpatient treatment being received. Even when involuntary commitment is pursued, it may not result in hospitalization if a psychiatric evaluation determines that there is no imminent risk. For example, a student who verbalizes suicidal threats may subsequently report no longer having suicidal intentions by the time of the evaluation (which often occurs when students have to wait long periods before being evaluated). A student who makes a serious suicide attempt will most likely be admitted. Once admitted, a student will be kept in the hospital for a minimum amount of time until discharged, after which follow-up care will usually be provided. Students are often started on psychotropic medication or have current medication use reevaluated when they are hospitalized.

An important consideration in hospitalizing students is whether to involve the parents. As discussed in Chapter 1, the issue that needs to be considered is whether notifying parents will help or potentially place a student at even greater risk. Parents can be helpful in a number of ways, such as determining whether the student should be hospitalized near home or the campus and in decisions regarding the student's academics (e.g., need to withdraw from courses, contacting professors, etc.). Decisions about whether to involve parents can be complicated by the fact that many students are on their parents' health care plans. Thus, parents may ultimately have knowledge of their adult child being hospitalized, but not necessarily at the time of the hospitalization.

Depending on the circumstances, a university may or may not have knowledge of one of their students being evaluated or hospitalized in an inpatient psychiatric unit or facility. When a student voluntarily admits him or herself without the assistance of anyone at the college, the hospital or facility may be precluded from notifying the school upon discharging the student. Although not necessarily standard protocol, many hospitals will seek the student's permission to forward pertinent medical records (typically to the counseling center) to assist in arranging for follow-up care on campus.

Crisis Response Teams

Many schools will have a crisis response plan prepared in the event of a campus crisis. This will typically involve a crisis response team (Eaves, 2001). When in place, such a team will consist of individuals with different types of knowledge or skills for responding to emergencies. Although this can include an assortment of individuals, it will usually consist of representatives from counseling, student health, campus police, and the dean of students' office. The primary task of a crisis response team is to help students and staff members cope in the aftermath of a crisis or critical incident occurring on or off campus. The specific tasks will vary depending on the type of incident but often will involve providing accurate information about the crisis event, helping to manage acute stress reactions, helping to manage fears and contain panic, and ensuring the health and safety of those on campus.

When a crisis or traumatic event occurs on campus, it can have a devastating effect on students and others in the campus community. The impact might be buffered by a number of factors such as the size of the campus and how many students are directly affected. Traumatic incidents can occur in many different ways. One of the more common forms of trauma to a campus occurs in the wake of a student suicide or serious suicide attempt. This can be especially traumatizing when other students witness the suicidal act or are present in the immediate aftermath of the attempted or completed suicide.

A student death from an accident or illness is another form of campus trauma, though the number of students affected can vary depending on the particular circumstances. As an example, emergency bereavement counseling was initiated following the sudden death of a first-year student from meningitis. Because this occurred relatively early in the new school year, intervention was primarily aimed at students in the residence where the deceased student had lived. However, the number of students affected became much greater after it was discovered that just before her death the young woman had attended a party at which beer was consumed by dozens of students from a shared, handheld spigot that was placed directly into their mouths. As a result, there was considerable fear and panic among those students who had drank from the spigot. A crisis response team consisting of counseling and medical personnel on campus was utilized to contain fears and provide information about symptoms of meningitis and the need for proper testing.

A crisis response team may need to respond to events that occur off campus as well. Traumatic events that occur in the surrounding community are likely to have reverberating effects on a campus, especially if students are involved. A prime example of a campus traumatized by what was happening in the surrounding community was the highly publicized and sensationalized serial murders of five University of Florida students in their off-campus apartments in 1990. The murders caused heightened anxieties (Biernat & Herkov, 1994) and required a significant amount of crisis management and rumor control to contain widespread fear and panic (Archer, 1992). Campuses also need to be prepared to respond in the aftermath of natural disasters such as tornadoes and earthquakes (McCarthy & Butler, 2003). Even a national or international event that occurs well beyond the confines of a campus can have a significant impact on the lives of people on campus. For example, many students experienced post-traumatic stress symptoms in the aftermath of the September 11 terrorist attacks (Cardenas, Williams, Wilson, Fanouraki, & Singh, 2003) and subsequent media exposure (DeRoma et al., 2003).

WITHDRAWAL AND READMISSION

Sometimes students with psychological problems are simply not equipped to handle the demands and pressures of academic life and need to consider the option of temporary or permanent withdrawal from school. In some instances troubled students need to be evaluated because they prompt concern about their capacity for remaining on campus, particularly following displays of disruptive behavior. A dean or other administrative official will ordinarily request such an evaluation, which is often conducted by a group or team of campus personnel who assess a student's situation and make recommendations. Such groups may go by various names, such as Student Assessment Team or Disruptive Behavior Assessment Team. The primary purpose of these evaluations is to determine how the university can assist troubled students to enhance their chances for success within the academic environment but ultimately may serve to determine the feasibility of their remaining in school.

Voluntary Withdrawal

Some students come to recognize on their own that they need to leave school, perhaps temporarily, because of emotional or psychological difficulties that interfere with their academic or social functioning. Other students may come to this realization with the assistance of individuals such as a trusted advisor or counselor. Regardless of how the decision is made, there are clearly cases when students can benefit from voluntarily taking some time off or away from school. When deciding to voluntarily withdraw, students need to determine how they can most meaningfully spend the time off from school. Some students that voluntarily withdraw because of emotional problems will use the time to engage in counseling or therapy in a more intensive manner than would have been possible while in college.

Colleges generally allow students to withdraw temporarily because of difficulties functioning in the academic setting and then subsequently reenroll (Meilman et al., 1992). This will often be documented as a medical leave or withdrawal, allowing student status to be maintained. Institutional policies may vary somewhat in the specifics of this process. At some schools, a medical leave for psychological or personal concerns will need to be officially granted by a dean or other administrative official. As such, students may need to provide documented support for the need for a medical leave from a staff member of the counseling center or an outside mental health professional. Even when a medical leave is granted at the student's request, the student may be strongly urged and perhaps expected to participate in counseling with a mental health professional before returning to school as a condition of the leave. This will depend on the nature and severity of the student's problems or condition and the circumstances prompting the request for a leave. Under these conditions, the student may subsequently need to provide evidence of having successfully participated in treatment.

Evidence does suggest that academic performance can be enhanced upon return from a temporary withdrawal for mental health reasons. Grade point averages have been found to rise significantly after return from such a leave (Meilman & Turco, 1995; Wiener & Wiener, 1997). Unfortunately, some students with emotional problems end up being academically dismissed due to poor performance. This is important for students to consider when they experience emotional distress that significantly interferes with academic functioning. Sometimes it is best to leave school temporarily in order to avoid academic failure and to enhance one's chances for improvement in the future.

Involuntary Withdrawal

Unlike voluntary withdrawal, the dismissal of students with mental health disturbances on an involuntary or mandatory basis can pose legal and ethical considerations. An involuntary withdrawal will typically be used as a last resort after all alternatives have been explored. Involuntary withdrawals are typically imposed in situations in which a student engages or threatens to engage in behavior that poses a danger to self or others or is significantly disruptive to others and/or the educational process. This includes suicidal behavior, threats of harm to others, psychotic behavior, substance abuse, and eating disorders that could have serious medical consequences.

According to DiScala, Olswang, and Niccolls (1992), universities have the authority to regulate student conduct and activity as a means of preserving order and safety on campus and preventing interference with the educational process. At the same time, administrators need to make certain that mandatory withdrawal procedures are used appropriately because of the potential for infringement on students' due-process rights (Coll, 1991; DiScala et al., 1992). For example, policies and procedures need to be well publicized so that students are fully aware of the expectations regarding their conduct and of the potential consequences of violations (Leach & Sewell, 1986). Kiracofe (1993) recommended that an administrative decision to remove a student be based on a combination of policy, staff recommendations, and the "best interests of all involved." Administrators have to walk a fine line between individual student rights and preserving safety and well-being within the campus community. What is best for a student may not be best for the institution, and administrators need to be accountable to the larger university community.

Disciplinary action for violations of the standards or code for student conduct is generally imposed with few complications when emotional disturbance does not appear to be a factor. When disciplinary sanctions are imposed for students with emotional problems, however, the situation may be more complicated. Clear and well-defined policy is extremely important in the administrative removal of students who are deemed high risk or become disruptive on campus due to mental health problems (Dannells & Stuber, 1992; Leach & Sewell, 1986). Reliance on "administrative decision models" can also be critical in the consideration of the dismissal of students with serious emotional disturbance (Gehring, 1984).

Leach and Sewell (1986) recommended that when using policy regarding the dismissal of students due to mental health problems, it must be clear that

1. the student violated standards of conduct, significantly interfered with the academic process, or posed a threat to the safety of any persons;
2. the conduct occurred as a result of a mental health condition or impairment; and
3. no other reasonable alternatives were available that could assure individual safety and/or prevent continued disruptions.

Amada (1992) contended that the use of mandatory psychological withdrawals should be avoided whenever dealing with disruptive students. He suggested that universities should impose a suspension or expulsion strictly based on the student's disruptive behavior as long as the following conditions can be demonstrated:

1. the student's behavior is having a significantly negative effect on other students and/or staff;
2. disciplinary sanctions have been imposed on the student for the harm that has been inflicted on others; and
3. the student continues to engage in the behavior after sanctions are imposed.

Cases involving potentially suicidal students can be particularly challenging for administrators. When every effort has been made to ensure that a student receives proper mental health care yet he or she continues to engage in suicidal behavior despite such efforts, then the only alternative may be for the institution to invoke an involuntary withdrawal. A few years ago I was asked by an administrative official to evaluate a student who requested to be allowed to remain on campus after having made a suicidal gesture by ingesting several nonprescription pills. The administrator wanted to make sure that this student was not going to pose a risk for further suicidal behavior if allowed to remain on campus. When I first met with the student, he said he no longer had any thoughts of suicide and characterized the gesture as a "stupid. mistake." He expressed motivation for using counseling to address issues that precipitated the suicidal behavior. Based on my interview with him, I informed the administrator that there was no real evidence to suggest that he posed any further risk and certainly no evidence to support an involuntary withdrawal. However, I did recommend that the decision to allow him to remain enrolled be contingent upon his using ongoing counseling, which he seemed most willing to do anyway.

I wish I could say that things went smoothly after that, but unfortunately that was not the case. He kept his first two counseling appointments but then began to be irregular in his attendance. He was not always responsive to my attempts to contact him when he missed appointments and would sometimes need to be seen on an unscheduled or walk-in basis. There were also indications that he was causing problems for others in his residence, especially his roommate. Based on reports from other students, evidence emerged to suggest that he was using illicit drugs and stealing some of his roommate's prescribed medicine. Because I had the prerogative to communicate with the administrative official who originally requested the evaluation, I conveyed my concerns about the student's irregular attendance in counseling, which in and of itself was a breach of the contract he agreed to as a condition to remain enrolled. The administrator also became aware of his disruptive behavior in his residence from other sources. As his case was in the process of being reevaluated, the student made a second suicidal gesture, this time making cuts on his wrist that necessitated medical attention in the campus health center. This incident was the culminating event which ultimately resulted in the decision to have him involuntarily withdrawn from the university.

This example shows how difficult cases involving suicidal risk can be and how important it is for a school to continue to monitor the progress of high-risk students when they are allowed to remain on campus. This is also a sobering example of how a screening interview cannot be used to reliably predict the likelihood of high-risk or troublesome behavior in the future (Hoffman & Mastrianni, 1991).

The difficult issue of involuntary withdrawal can also arise when dealing with students with severe eating disorders. A student with an eating disorder may come to the attention of an administrative official because of concerns conveyed by others about the student's physical health and well-being. Medical concerns typically arise in cases of anorexia when a student's weight can become unsafe or unstable. In such cases the student may be required to be monitored medically and asked to agree to a contract in which the student's weight cannot drop below a specific point. If the weight goes below the specified level, the student would need to take a medical leave from school. At some schools an eating disorder treatment team consisting of representatives from counseling and health services (and a nutritionist, if available) might conduct this type of monitoring. Students with severe eating disorders may simply need more intensive care than what can be provided on campus. Students with eating disorders might also prompt a disciplinary response and possible withdrawal if the behavior is disruptive to others (e.g., frequent vomiting in public restrooms or stealing food from roommates).

Conditions for Readmission

After a student is granted a medical leave or is involuntarily withdrawn, a procedure should be in place for the student to be evaluated for readmission. This will typically consist of a screening interview conducted by the dean of students and/or the director (or designated representative) of campus counseling. On many campuses, an assessment team might be used to make recommendations to the dean or other administrative official. The primary intention of the evaluation is to assess the student's readiness to return to school. Resuming academic study can often be helpful for students as they continue treatment for emotional and psychological difficulties, but this needs to be weighed against possible effects to other students and the campus as a whole (Gift & Southwick, 1988; Hoffmann & Mastrianni, 1991).

Hoffmann and Mastrianni (1991) noted that campus policies could vary in terms of defining procedures for reentry following an absence for psychological reasons. Schools may set requirements for a minimum amount of time out of school before returning, usually one semester to a full year. Some schools may not only require a student to provide evidence of having participated in therapy during the period of being out of school but also for the student to be in treatment upon returning to school.

Concerns have been raised about students being readmitted prematurely in terms of the readiness of the affected student and/or impact on others within the campus community (Gift & Southwick, 1988; Meilman et al., 1992). Students and their parents may exude considerable pressure on schools to allow for a return to campus much sooner than the school is comfortable with, perhaps because they perceive the campus environment as somehow being better for the student than living at home. In a discussion of premature readmissions for students following a psychotic break, Gift and Southwick noted how students and their families might hold unrealistic expectations about the therapeutic value of academic study. Off-campus mental health professionals who provide treatment to students while they are out of school have also been known to favor students making a quick return to school without necessarily considering the impact on the campus community. This may be simply due to the fact that outside professionals will typically not have knowledge of the specific dynamics of a particular campus culture.

Although the intentions of family and off-campus therapists may be driven by what they think is best for the student, a premature readmission can have potentially troublesome consequences (Meilman et al., 1992), as the following example illustrates. A student made a very serious suicide attempt at the end of a fall semester and then subsequently requested to resume academic study the following spring, which would have amounted to about a four-week interval between the suicide attempt and return to school. Aside from concerns about the student's continuing level of risk given such a relatively short interval, there were concerns about the impact of the student's return on other students such as friends, roommates, and teammates. Several of the student's peers were traumatized by the suicide attempt because they witnessed it at a social gathering. Many of these peers protested when they learned about the student wanting to return to school so soon after the suicide attempt.

Based on the seriousness of the suicide attempt and the concerns of other students, the request for readmission for the spring term was denied on the grounds that it was not sufficient enough time to ensure that the student was no longer at risk and that it would create considerable anxiety for several other students. The student was encouraged to apply for readmission after a full semester out of school. In addition, consideration of readmission was to be based on the student providing documentation from a licensed mental health professional confirming the student's participation in treatment and providing support for a return to school.

It is natural for administrative officials to rely on their own campus counseling center staff members for the process of evaluating students for readmission, yet objections have been made about the use of counseling staff in readmission evaluations (Amada, 1986, 1992; Gilbert, 1989; Hoffman & Mastrianni, 1991; Kiracofe, 1993). These objections tend to be based on two issues. First, students that are readmitted are often required to use counseling on campus; consequently, this can pose potential complications for the counseling relationship when counseling centers play a role in recommendations for students to be in counseling. Second, as Kiracofe explained, this could create problems with the image that students have of campus counseling, particularly in terms of their perceptions of how well confidentiality is maintained.

Gilbert suggested that counseling centers should simply help administrators evaluate the evidence that is provided by outside mental health professionals regarding students' readiness to return to school. However, as noted earlier, outside mental health professionals may too easily recommend a student's return without considering other issues within the larger campus community simply because they are not a part of it. As Widseth et al. (1997) have noted, it may be unrealistic to rely solely upon outside evaluators to balance the needs and resources of both the individual student and the institution. Despite some valid objections, administrators have continued to use campus counseling staff in the readmission process and thus counseling centers need to do what they can to prevent this role from tarnishing their image or interfering in their delivery of services.

MANDATORY COUNSELING

Many colleges use mandatory counseling as a disciplinary sanction or condition for students to remain in or return to school or a residence hall. It continues to be common practice for administrative officials to impose counseling as a condition of continued enrollment for students who violate standards of conduct. Students are mandated to counseling following incidents of alcohol and drug abuse, alcohol policy violations, violence, harassment, and other disciplinary infractions. This seems to be based on the idea that many forms of disruptive or troublesome behavior involve underlying emotional issues such as poor impulse control, depression, anger, stress, and interpersonal difficulties (Dannells, 1990). Students may also be required to be in counseling because of behavior associated with specific types of emotional disturbance, particularly if it places students at risk or is disruptive to others. When counseling is mandated, students usually fulfill this by using campus counseling services but may have the option of receiving counseling off campus. In either case, students will be expected to secure an appropriate release so that the counselor can verify attendance and, if requested, submit an evaluation or progress report.

Following a judicial hearing or evaluation requested by an administrative official, students are sent a letter informing them of any disciplinary sanctions, which might include mandatory counseling. An example of a letter based on a judicial hearing for an alcohol violation might be as follows:

Dear Student:
    A hearing was conducted to address your involvement in the incident that occurred on March 1, 2004. Based on the evidence presented, the panel found you responsible for a violation of the University Code of Conduct alcohol standard. As a result, you are being placed on disciplinary probation for one semester effective immediately. During this time period you may not hold office in any student organization, participate in athletic competition, or otherwise represent the University.
    In addition, you are hereby directed to meet with a counselor in the University Counseling Center for an alcohol assessment and any follow-up counseling recommended by the counselor. You are to continue in this program of counseling until such time that both you and the counselor agree. Please be advised that when you meet with the counselor, you are to sign appropriate releases and information is to be forthcoming back to this office regarding your progress. Failure to complete this sanction will result in your potential dismissal from the University.
    Subsequent violations of the Code of Conduct while on disciplinary probation are also likely to result in your dismissal from the University.

It is the hope of the panel that you will take every precaution to prevent that from happening.

Sincerely,

Director of Student Conduct

College administrators have increasingly relied on counseling centers to assist in the management and treatment of disruptive students. Just as there has been opposition to the use of counseling centers in readmission decisions, strong arguments have also been made against coercively referring students for counseling. Several authors (Amada, 1992; Dannells & Consolvo, 2000; Gilbert, 1989; Gilbert & Sheiman, 1995; Kiracofe, 1993; Stone & Lucas, 1994) have stressed that mandatory counseling is overused, clinically inadvisable, ethically and legally questionable, and unlikely to be effective. Gilbert and Sheiman characterized mandatory counseling as rarely justifiable because counseling seldom works with students who are unmotivated, not ready, expect little from it, and resent being in it. Likewise, Dannells and Consolvo contended that mandatory counseling will not necessarily produce any significant behavior change because students can simply tell counselors what they want to hear just to end the counseling requirement. Morgan and Cavendish (1987) voiced similar arguments against mandatory counseling for students who get in trouble for alcohol- and drug-related infractions. Such concerns leave many college counselors seeing mandatory counseling as an ineffective use of resources, especially when there is a high demand for services from students seeking help voluntarily.

Concerns have also been expressed about a counseling center serving as a disciplinary office or unofficial enforcer for the school's administration, which could damage its integrity and reputation as an impartial entity within the university (Francis, 2000; Gilbert, 1989). Even the International Association of Counseling Services states that a counseling center should be "administratively neutral" and maintain no disciplinary function or power within the institution because this could compromise counseling services (Boyd et al., 2003).

The use of disciplinary "education" has been advocated as a more effective alternative to mandatory counseling and one that is less likely to harm the reputation of the counseling center (Dannells & Consolvo, 2000; Gilbert & Sheiman, 1995; Morgan & Cavendish, 1987; Stone &

Lucas, 1994). This entails requiring students to attend an educational session or program (possibly in a group format) in which they are provided with information and suggestions but not expected to disclose personal information. Examples include educational sessions or programs for responsible alcohol use, anger management, values clarification, and making responsible choices and decisions. Morgan and Cavendish (1987) proposed that disciplinary education was a particularly effective means of responding to students who violate the school's alcohol policy but show no evidence of serious problems. One example might be students who engage in underage drinking violations.

Despite the concerns of college counselors about the practice of mandatory counseling, it persists as an administrative response and means of handling troubled and disruptive students. As Francis (2000) articulated, college counselors need to be responsive to administrative needs and work collaboratively to provide a safe campus environment for students. Though I agree with many of the arguments made against mandatory counseling, I agree with Francis that this is an important means of being responsive to administrators who have the unenviable task of dealing with troublesome students on campus. I truly believe that some students can potentially benefit in significant ways even when participation is mandated. If the practice of mandating counseling is going to have any chance for success, clear and mutually agreed upon guidelines will need to be established between administrators and counselors (Dannells & Consolvo, 2000; Francis, 2000).

LIMITATIONS OF CAMPUS COUNSELING

Campus counseling is an important component of student services, yet does have its limitations. The treatment needs of some students exceed typical counseling center resources (Gilbert, 1992). For example, some students require frequent contacts or more intensive work than can be offered on a limited basis. Gilbert argued that trying to provide counseling in such cases might raise ethical and legal concerns: "It is misguided kindness, as well as being ethically unwise and legally risky, to attempt to carry out a treatment mission with inadequate resources" (p. 698). Trying to provide counseling to a small proportion of students who demand a large percentage of time can also place a strain on resources that may already be limited.

Campus counseling services may not be appropriate for some students for other reasons. Amada (1999) described how some students attempt to use counseling in a manner that is either inappropriate or possibly disruptive. For example, students may have illegitimate reasons for being in counseling or may be disrespectful or even abusive toward counseling center staff. Under such circumstances, students may need to be disqualified or excluded from utilizing counseling services on campus.

When students are deemed to be inappropriate for on-campus counseling, arrangements will typically be made to refer them to off-campus resources (LaCour & Carter, 2002). With short-term counseling becoming the norm, some students need to be referred off-campus when they reach the limit of counseling that can be received on campus. LaCour and Carter provide an examination of the challenges and obstacles involved in trying to make off-campus referrals.

SUMMARY

Colleges have developed and implemented policies and practices for responding to specific issues related to student mental health. The most common policies address means for evaluating and providing accommodations to students with psychological disabilities, responding to psychological emergencies, conditions for voluntary or involuntary withdrawal from school, and the use of mandatory counseling. College counselors typically play a key role in all of these dimensions of responding to issues of student mental health. Although campus counseling is a valuable asset in helping schools cope with troubled students, there are limitations in the scope of services that can be responsibly provided within the campus setting.

Conclusion

Effectively responding to students in distress requires collaboration. College counselors do bear the primary responsibility for addressing the mental health needs of students on campus, yet the success of their efforts is based in part on how well they collaborate with others within the campus community. As I have stressed throughout this resource guide, it is critical that all individuals who work on a college campus be aware of and attentive to students who may be experiencing psychological distress. Many students in distress will not seek counseling assistance on their own, and thus it is incumbent upon college personnel to do what they can to ensure that troubled students receive proper attention and mental health care.

In addition to helping others in the campus community learn to identify and refer students in distress, I have found that strong and positive working relationships between counselors and others on campus is a key factor in effectively responding to troubled students. College campuses are communities with a myriad of resources for students. Having knowledge of the various resources and student support services on campus is clearly important, but good communication within and across different offices and departments may be even more important. It is one thing to inform students of services that they can benefit from, yet another thing altogether when it comes to what students do with that information. Especially when dealing with emotionally troubled students, there is a strong likelihood that they will not seek or follow through on getting help unless people on campus are proactive in assisting them to do so.

In my years of experience, the process of helping distressed students has been most effective when others on campus not only refer students to counseling but also provide essential background information to counselors regarding the circumstances that aroused concern. It can also help when others are active in assisting students with scheduling appointments or even escorting them to the counseling of-

College Students in Distress
© 2006 by The Haworth Press, Inc. All rights reserved.
doi:10.1300/5228_08

fice in some cases. Some students will simply not take any initiative without the active efforts of concerned others. Likewise, college counselors often need to refer students to other support services on campus and can play an active role in helping students to access and utilize these other services. With student consent, counselors often communicate with people in other campus offices in order to help students receive assistance with academics and other issues such as financial aid and housing. I find that it increases the chances of students benefiting from the availability of such services when I make contact with people in these other offices before referring students. I will also contact other resource people who may be able to help without students needing to be referred, for example, to clarify an issue or obtain information for a student.

The pace of life on a typical college campus does pose challenges to faculty and staff members in their efforts to communicate with one another regarding students in distress. However, colleges cannot afford to risk responding inadequately to troubled students. This is particularly true in cases of apparent warning signs of suicide given the increase in liability (Franke, 2004). I have seen many students fall through the cracks when communication was poor or nonexistent. Aside from preventing or reducing institutional liability, colleges generally bear a significant degree of responsibility for ensuring the safety and well-being of their students. Although it is inevitable that some troubled students will go unidentified, especially on larger campuses, the concerted efforts of those who work with students can dramatically lessen this from happening.

The increased attention to student mental health in recent years is likely to result in enhanced efforts for strong collaboration on campuses across the country. This may entail cluster groups or task forces devoted specifically to addressing the mental health care of students or perhaps opportunities for counselors to exchange ideas and information with faculty and staff members. Working together, college personnel can be proactive in meeting the growing demand for mental health care for students. It is my hope that this guide will contribute to this effort.

References

Allen, D.R., & Trimble, R.W. (1993). Identifying and referring troubled students: A primer for academic advisors. *NACADA Journal, 13,* 34-41.

Amada, G. (1986). Dealing with disturbed college students: Some theoretical and practical considerations. *Journal of American College Health, 34,* 221-225.

Amada, G. (1992). Coping with the disruptive college student: A practical model. *Journal of American College Health, 40,* 203-215.

Amada, G. (1993). The role of the mental health consultant in dealing with disruptive college students. *Journal of College Student Psychotherapy, 8,* 121-137.

Amada, G. (1999). Disqualifying specified students from the campus psychological service: Some considerations and guidelines. *Journal of College Student Psychotherapy, 13,* 7-24.

Amada, G., & Grayson, P.A. (1989). Anxiety. In P.A. Grayson & K. Cauley (Eds.), *College psychotherapy* (pp. 150-165). New York: Guilford Press.

Americans with Disabilities Act of 1990, 42 U.S.C.A. § 12101 *et seq.* (West 1993).

Archer, J. (1991). *Counseling college students: A practical guide for teachers, parents, and counselors.* New York: Continuum Publishing.

Archer, J. (1992). Campus in crisis: Coping with fear and panic related to serial murders. *Journal of Counseling and Development, 71,* 96-100.

Arnstein, R.L. (1989). Chronically disturbed students. In P.A. Grayson & K. Cauley (Eds.), *College psychotherapy* (pp. 29-47). New York: Guilford Press.

Attie, I., Brooks-Gunn, J., & Petersen, A.C. (1990). A developmental perspective on eating disorders and eating problems. In M. Lewis & S.M. Miller (Eds.), *Handbook of developmental psychopathology* (pp. 409-420). New York: Plenum Press.

Backels, K., & Wheeler, I. (2001). Faculty perceptions of mental health issues among college students. *Journal of College Student Development, 42,* 173-176.

Barkin, C. (1999). *When your kid goes to college.* New York: Avon Books.

Bartlett, T. (2002, February 1). Freshmen pay, mentally and physically, as they adjust to life in college. *The Chronicle of Higher Education, 48,* p. A35.

Benton, S.A., Robertson, J.M., Tseng, W.C., Newton, F.B., & Benton, S.L. (2003). Changes in counseling center client problems across 13 years. *Professional Psychology: Research and Practice, 34,* 66-72.

Biernat, M., & Herkov, M.J. (1994). Reactions of violence: A campus copes with serial murders. *Journal of Social and Clinical Psychology, 13,* 309-334.

College Students in Distress
© 2006 by The Haworth Press, Inc. All rights reserved.
doi:10.1300/5228_09

Birky, I., Sharkin, B.S., Marin, J., & Scappaticci, A. (1998). Confidentiality after referral: A study of how restrictions on disclosure affect relationships between therapists and referral sources. *Professional Psychology: Research and Practice, 29,* 179-182.

Bishop, J.B. (2002). Students with histories of counseling: Implications for counseling centers and other administrative units. *Journal of College Student Development, 43,* 130-133.

Bishop, J.B., Bishop, K.A., & Beale, C.L. (1992). A longitudinal look at faculty knowledge and perceptions of a university counseling center. *Journal of College Student Development, 33,* 374-375.

Bombardieri, M. (2005, July 30). Lawsuit allowed in MIT suicide. *The Boston Globe.* Retrieved August 3, 2005, from http://www.boston.com.

Boswinkel, J.P. (1987). The college resident assistant (RA) and the fine art of referral for psychotherapy. *Journal of College Student Psychotherapy, 1,* 53-62.

Boyd, V., Hattauer, E., Brandel, I.W., Buckles, N., Davidshofer, C., Deakin, S., Erskine, C., Hurley, G., Lochler, L., Piorkowski, G., et al. (2003). Accreditation standards for university and college counseling centers. *Journal of Counseling and Development, 81,* 168-177.

Boyer, S.P., & Sedlacek, W.E. (1989). Non-cognitive predictors of counseling center use by international students. *Journal of Counseling and Development, 67,* 404-407.

Brackney, B.E., & Karabenick, S.A. (1995). Psychopathology and academic performance: The role of motivation and learning strategies. *Journal of Counseling Psychology, 42,* 456-465.

Bradley, L., Parr, G., Lan, W.Y., Bingi, R., & Gould, L.T. (1995). Counseling expectations of international students. *International Journal of the Advancement of Counselling, 18,* 21-31.

Brener, N.D., Hassan, S.S., & Barrios, L.C. (1999). Suicidal ideation among college students in the United States. *Journal of Clinical and Consulting Psychology, 67,* 1004-1008.

Brinson, J.A., & Kottler, J.A. (1995a). International students in counseling: Some alternative models. *Journal of College Student Psychotherapy, 9,* 57-70.

Brinson, J.A., & Kottler, J.A. (1995b). Minorities' underutilization of counseling centers' mental health services: A case for outreach and consultation. *Journal of Mental Health Counseling, 17,* 371-386.

Campus Care and Counseling Act, H.R. 3593, 108th Cong. (2003).

Campus Care and Counseling Act, S. 2215, 108th Cong. (2004).

Cardenas, J., Williams, K., Wilson, J.P., Fanouraki, G., & Singh, A. (2003). PTSD, major depressive symptoms, and substance abuse following September 11, 2001, in a midwestern university population. *International Journal of Emergency Mental Health, 5,* 15-28.

Carter, G.C., & Winseman, J.S. (2003). Increasing numbers of students arriving on college campuses on psychiatric medications: Are they mentally ill? *Journal of College Student Psychotherapy, 18,* 3-10.

Cashen, J.R., Presky, C.A., & Meilman, P.W. (1998). Alcohol use in the Greek system: Follow the leader? *Journal of Studies on Alcohol, 59,* 63-70.

Cheng, D., Leong, F.T.L., & Geist, R. (1993). Cultural differences in psychological distress between Asian and Caucasian American college students. *Journal of Multicultural Counseling and Development, 21,* 182-190.

Chung, I.W. (2003). Examining suicidal behavior of Asian American female college students: Implications for practice. *Journal of College Student Psychotherapy, 18,* 31-47.

Clark Oropeza, B.A., Fitzgibbon, M., & Baron, Jr., A. (1991). Managing mental health crises of foreign college students. *Journal of Counseling and Development, 69,* 280-284.

Clements, R. (1999). Prevalence of alcohol-use disorders and alcohol-related problems in a college student sample. *Journal of American College Health, 48,* 111-118.

Coburn, K.L., & Treeger, M.L. (1997). *Letting go: A parents' guide to understanding the college years.* New York: Harper Collins Publishers.

Cogan, K.D., & Petrie, T.A. (1996). Counseling college women student-athletes. In E.F. Etzel, A.P. Ferrante, & J.W. Pinkney (Eds.), *Counseling college student-athletes: Issues and interventions* (2nd ed., pp. 77-106). Morgantown, WV: Fitness Information Technology, Inc.

Coll, K.M. (1991). Mandatory psychiatric withdrawal from public colleges and universities: A review of potential legal violations and appropriate use. *Journal of College Student Psychotherapy, 5,* 91-98.

Collins, M.E., & Mowbray, C.T. (2005). Higher education and psychiatric disabilities: National survey of campus disability services. *American Journal of Orthopsychiatry, 75,* 304-315.

Constantine, M.G., Chen, E.C., & Ceesay, P. (1997). Intake concerns of racial and ethnic minority students at a university counseling center: Implications for developmental programming and outreach. *Journal of Multicultural Counseling and Development, 25,* 210-218.

Constantine, M.G., Wilton, L., & Caldwell, L.D. (2003). The role of social support in moderating the relationship between psychological distress and willingness to seek psychological help among black and Latino college students. *Journal of College Counseling, 6,* 155-165.

Corazzini, J.G., & Shelton, J. (1974). A conceptualization of the referral process. *Journal of College Student Personnel, 15,* 461-464.

Cornish, J.A., Kominars, K.D., Riva, M.T., McIntosh, S., & Henderson, M.C. (2000). Perceived distress in university counseling center clients across a six-year period. *Journal of College Student Development, 41,* 104-109.

Coulter, L.P., Offutt, C.A., & Mascher, J. (2003). Counseling center management of after-hours crises: Practice and problems. *Journal of College Student Psychotherapy, 18,* 11-34.

Council for the Advancement of Standards in Higher Education (2003). *The book of professional standards in higher education.* Washington, DC: Author.

Damm, J., & Murray, P. (1996). Alcohol and other drug use among college student-athletes. In E.F. Etzel, A.P. Ferrante, & J.W. Pinkney (Eds.), *Counseling college student-athletes: Issues and interventions* (2nd ed., pp. 185-220). Morgantown, WV: Fitness Information Technology, Inc.

Dannells, M. (1990). Changes in policies and practices over 10 years. *Journal of College Student Development, 31,* 408-414.

Dannells, M., & Consolvo, C. (2000). Disciplinary counseling: Implications for policy and practice. *NASPA Journal, 38,* 44-57.

Dannells, M., & Stuber, D. (1992). Mandatory psychiatric withdrawal of severely disturbed students: A study and policy recommendations. *NASPA Journal, 29,* 163-168.

D'Augelli, A.R. (1992). Lesbian and gay male undergraduates's experiences of harassment and fear on campus. *Journal of Interpersonal Violence, 7,* 383-395.

D'Augelli, A.R. (1993). Preventing mental health problems among lesbian and gay college students. *Journal of Primary Prevention, 13,* 245-261.

D'Augelli, A.R., & Rose, M.L. (1990). Homophobia in a university community: Attitudes and experiences of heterosexual freshmen. *Journal of College Student Development, 31,* 484-491.

Dean, L.A. (2000). College counseling today: Changing roles and definitions. In D.C. Davis & K.M. Humphrey (Eds.), *College counseling: Issues and strategies for a new millennium* (pp. 41-56). Alexandria, VA: American Counseling Association.

Deane, F.P., & Todd, D.M. (1996). Attitudes and intentions to seek professional psychological help for personal problems or suicidal thinking. *Journal of College Student Development, 10,* 45-59.

De Lucia, R.C., & Iasenza, S. (1995). Student disruption, disrespect, and disorder in class: A seminar for faculty. *Journal of College Student Development, 36,* 385-388.

DeRoma, V., Saylor, C., Swickert, R., Sinisi, C., Marable, T.B., & Vickery, P. (2003). College students' PTSD symptoms, coping, and perceived benefits following media exposure to 9/11. *Journal of College Student Psychotherapy, 18,* 49-64.

DiScala, J., Olswang, S.G., & Niccolls, C.S. (1992). College and university responses to the emotionally and mentally impaired student. *Journal of College and University Law, 19,* 17-33.

Dworkin, J. (2005). Risk taking as developmentally appropriate experimentation for college studetns. *Journal of Adolescent Research, 20,* 219-241.

Eaves, C. (2001). The development and implementation of a crisis response team in a school setting. *International Journal of Emergency Mental Health, 3,* 35-46.

Ellingson, K.T., Kochenour, E.O., & Weitzman, L.M. (1999). University counseling center consultation: Developing a faculty orientation program. *Consulting Psychology Journal: Practice and Research, 51,* 31-36.

Engs, R.C., Diebold, B.A., & Hanson, D.J. (1994). The drinking patterns and problems of a national sample of college students. *Journal of Alcohol and Drug Education, 41*, 13-33.

Foreman, M.E. (1990). The counselor's assessment and intervention with the suicidal student. *Journal of College Student Psychotherapy, 4*, 125-140.

Francis, P.C. (2000). Practicing ethically as a college counselor. In D.C. Davis & K.M. Humphrey (Eds.), *College counseling: Issues and strategies for a new millennium* (pp. 71-86). Alexandria, VA: American Counseling Association.

Francis, P.C. (2003). Developing ethical institutional policies and procedures for working with suicidal students on a college campus. *Journal of College Counseling, 6*, 114-123.

Franke, A.H. (2004, June 25). When students kill themselves, colleges may get the blame. *The Chronicle of Higher Education, 50*, pp. B18-B19.

Furr, S.R., Westefeld, J.S., McConnell, G.N., & Jenkins, J.M. (2001). Suicide and depression among college students: A decade later. *Professional Psychology: Research and Practice, 32*, 97-100.

Garrett Lee Smith Memorial Act, H.R. 4799, 108th Cong. (2004).

Garrett Lee Smith Memorial Act, S. 2674, 108th Cong. (2004).

Gehring, D.D. (1984). The dismissal of students with serious emotional problems: An administrative decision model. *NASPA Journal, 20*, 9-14.

Gibson, J.M. (2000). Documentation of emotional and mental disabilities: The role of the counseling center. *Journal of College Counseling, 3*, 63-72.

Gift, T., & Southwick, W. (1988). Premature return to school following a psychotic episode. *Journal of American College Health, 36*, 289-292.

Gilbert, S.P. (1989). The juggling act of the college counseling center: A point of view. *The Counseling Psychologist, 17*, 477-489.

Gilbert, S.P. (1992). Ethical issues in the treatment of severe psychopathology in university and college counseling centers. *Journal of Counseling and Development, 70*, 695-699.

Gilbert, S.P., & Sheiman, J.A. (1995). Mandatory counseling of university students: An oxymoron? *Journal of College Student Psychotherapy, 9*, 3-21.

Gladstone, T.R.G., & Koenig, L.J. (1994). Sex differences in depression across the high school to college transition. *Journal of Youth and Adolescence, 23*, 643-669.

Goode, E. (2003, February 3). More in college seek help for psychological problems. *The New York Times*, p. A11.

Goplerud, E.N. (1980). Social support and stress during the first year of graduate school. *Professional Psychology, 11*, 283-290.

Grant, K., Marsh, P., Syniar, G., Williams, M., Addlesperger, E., Kinzler, M.H., & Cowman, S. (2002). Gender differences in rates of depression among undergraduates: Measurement matters. *Journal of Adolescence, 25*, 613-617.

Gratz, K.L., Conrad, S.D., & Roemer, L. (2002). Risk factors for deliberate self-harm among college students. *American Journal of Orthopsychiatry, 72*, 128-140.

Grayson, P., Schwartz, V., & Commerford, M. (1997). Brave new world? Drug therapy and college mental health. *Journal of College Student Psychotherapy, 11,* 23-55.

Green, B.C. (1998). Thinking about students who do not identify as gay, lesbian, or bisexual, but . . . *Journal of American College Health, 47,* 89-91.

Grosz, R.D. (1991). Suicide: Training the resident assistant as an interventionist. *Journal of College Student Psychotherapy, 4,* 179-194.

Haas, A.P., Hendin, H., & Mann, J.J. (2003). Suicide in college students. *American Behavioral Scientist, 46,* 1224-1240.

Haines, M.E., Norris, M.P., & Kashy, D.A. (1996). The effects of depressed mood on academic performance in college students. *Journal of College Student Development, 37,* 519-526.

Harris, R.S. (2002). Dual relationships and university counseling center environments. In A.A. Lazarus & O. Zur (Eds.), *Dual relationships and psychotherapy* (pp. 337- 347). New York: Springer Publishing.

Hayes, R.L., & Lin, H.-R. (1994). Coming to America: Developing social support systems for international students. *Journal of Multicultural Counseling and Development, 22,* 7-16.

Hernandez, T.J., & Fister, D.L. (2001). Dealing with disruptive and emotional college students: A systems model. *Journal of College Counseling, 4,* 49-62.

Hinkle, J.S. (1996). Depression, adjustment disorder, generalized anxiety, and substance abuse: An overview for sport professionals working with college student-athletes. In E.F. Etzel, A.P. Ferrante, & J.W. Pinkney (Eds.), *Counseling college student-athletes: Issues and interventions* (2nd ed., pp. 109-136). Morgantown, WV: Fitness Information Technology, Inc.

Hodges, S. (2001). University counseling centers at the twenty-first century: Looking forward, looking back. *Journal of College Counseling, 4,* 161-173.

Hodgson, C.S., & Simoni, J.M. (1995). Graduate student academic and psychological functioning. *Journal of College Student Development, 36,* 244-253.

Hoffmann, F.L., & Mastrianni, X. (1991). Psychiatric leave policies: Myth and reality. *Journal of College Student Psychotherapy, 6,* 3-20.

Horning, A. (1998). Helping students in trouble. *College Teaching, 46,* 2-6.

Iosupovici, M., & Luke, E. (2002). College and university student counseling centers: Inevitable boundary shifts and dual roles. In A.A. Lazarus & O. Zur (Eds.), *Dual relationships and psychotherapy* (pp. 360-378). New York: Springer Publishing.

Jacobs, E., & Glater, S. (1993). Students, staff, and community: A collaborative model of college services for students with psychological disabilities. *Psychosocial Rehabilitation Journal, 17,* 201-209.

Johnson, C., Powers, P.S., & Dick, R. (1999). Athletes and eating disorders: The National Collegiate Athletic Association study. *International Journal of Eating Disorders, 26,* 179-188.

Johnson, H.E. (2004, January 9). Educating parents about college life. *The Chronicle of Higher Education, 50,* p. B11.

Johnson, H.E., & Schelhas-Miller, C. (2000). *Don't tell me what to do, just send money: The essential parenting guide to the college years.* New York: St. Martin's Press.

Juhnke, G.A., Schroat, D.A., Cashwell, C.S., & Gmutza, B.M. (2003). A preliminary investigation of college students' alcohol consumption at two universities with limited Greek systems. *Journal of Addictions and Offender Counseling, 24,* 35-45.

Kahn, J.H., & Nauta, M.N. (1997). The influence of student problem-solving appraisal and nature of problem on likelihood of seeking counseling services. *Journal of College Student Development, 38,* 32-39.

Kahn, J.H., & Williams, M.N. (2003). The impact of prior counseling on predictors of college counseling center use. *Journal of College Counseling, 6,* 144-154.

Kelly, A.E., & Achter, J.A. (1995). Self-concealment and attitudes toward counseling in university students. *Journal of Counseling Psychology, 42,* 40-46.

Kennedy, A. (2004). NYU counseling director defends services, students in suicide media blitz. *Counseling Today, 46,* 28.

Kessler, R.C., Foster, C.L., Saunders, W.B., & Stang, P.E. (1995). Social consequences of psychiatric disorders: I. Educational attainment. *American Journal of Psychiatry, 152,* 1026-1032.

Kiracofe, N.M. (1993). Changing demands on counseling centers: Problems and possibilities. *Journal of College Student Psychotherapy, 7,* 69-83.

Kirn, W. (2003, November 3). University blues: A crisis. *Time, 162,* p. 55.

Kitzrow, M.A. (2003). The mental health needs of today's college students: Challenges and recommendations. *NASPA Journal, 41,* 165-179.

Kluger, J. (2003, November 3). Medicating young minds. *Time, 162,* pp. 48-58.

Lacour, M.M., & Carter, E.F. (2002). Challenges of referral decisions in college counseling. *Journal of College Student Psychotherapy, 17,* 39-52.

Lamb, C.S. (1992). Managing disruptive college students: The mental health practitioner as a consultant for faculty and staff. *Journal of College Student Psychotherapy, 7,* 23-39.

Leach, B.E., & Sewell, J.D. (1986). Responding to students with mental disorders: A framework for action. *NASPA Journal, 22,* 37-43.

Leichliter, J.S., Meilman, P.W., Presley, C.A., & Cashin, J.R. (1998). Alcohol use and related consequences among students with varying levels of involvement in college athletics. *Journal of American College Health, 46,* 257-262.

Leong, F.T.L., Wagner, N.S., & Tata, S.P. (1995). Racial and ethnic variations in help-seeking attitudes. In J.G. Ponterotto, J.M. Casas, L.A. Suzuki, & C.M. Alexander (Eds.), *Handbook of multicultural counseling* (pp. 415-438). Thousand Oaks, CA: Sage.

Lin, J.-C.G. (2000). College counseling and international students. In D.C. Davis & K.M. Humphrey (Eds.), *College counseling: Issues and strategies for a new millennium* (pp. 169-183). Alexandria, VA: American Counseling Association.

Lott, J.K., Ness, M.E., Alcorn, J.S., & Greer, R.M. (1999). The impact of gender and age on referrals to psychological counseling. *Journal of Counseling Psychology, 46,* 132-136.

Malley, P., Gallagher, R., & Brown, S.M. (1992). Ethical problems in university and college counseling centers: A Delphi Study. *Journal of College Student Development, 33,* 238-244.

Martinez, A.M., Huang, K.H., Johnson, Jr., S.D., & Edwards, Jr., S. (1989). Ethnic and international students. In P.A. Grayson & K. Cauley (Eds.), *College Psychotherapy* (pp. 298-315). New York: Guilford Press.

McCarthy, M.A., & Butler, L. (2003). Responding to traumatic events on college campuses: A case study and assessment of student post disaster anxiety. *Journal of College Counseling, 6,* 90-96.

McDermott, D., Tyndall, L., & Lichtenberg, J.W. (1989). Factors related to counselor preference among gays and lesbians. *Journal of Counseling and Development, 68,* 31-35.

Meadows, M.E. (2000). The evolution of college counseling. In D.C. Davis & K.M. Humphrey (Eds.), *College counseling: Issues and strategies for a new millennium* (pp. 15-40). Alexandria, VA: American Counseling Association.

Megivern, D., Pellerito, S., & Mowbray, C. (2003). Barriers to higher education for individuals with psychiatric disabilities. *Psychiatric Rehabilitation Journal, 26,* 217- 231.

Meilman, P.W., & Gaylor, M.S. (1989). Substance abuse. In P.A. Grayson & K. Cauley (Eds.), *College psychotherapy* (pp. 193-215). New York: Guilford Press.

Meilman, P.W., Gaylor, M.S., Turco, J.H., & Stone, J.E. (1990). Drug use among college undergraduates: Current use and 10-year trends. *International Journal of the Addictions, 25,* 1025-1036.

Meilman, P.W., Hacker, D.S., & Kraus-Zeilmann, D. (1993). Use of the mental health on-call system on a university campus. *Journal of American College Health, 42,* 105-109.

Meilman, P.W., Leichliter, J.S., & Presley, C.A. (1999). Greeks and athletes: Who drinks more? *Journal of American College Health, 47,* 187-190.

Meilman, P.W., Manley, C., Gaylor, M.S., & Turco, J.H. (1992). Medical withdrawals from college for mental health reasons and their relation to academic performance. *Journal of American College Health, 40,* 217-223.

Meilman, P.W., Pattis, J.A., & Kraus-Zeilmann, D. (1994). Suicide attempts and threats on one college campus: Policy and practice. *Journal of American College Health, 42,* 147-154.

Meilman, P.W., Presley, C.A., & Cashin, J.R. (1997). Average weekly alcohol consumption: Drinking percentiles for American college students. *Journal of American College Health, 45,* 201-204.

Meilman, P.W., Stone, J.E., Gaylor, M.S., & Truco, J.H. (1990). Alcohol consumption by college undergraduates: Current use and 10-year trends. *Journal of Studies on Alcohol, 51,* 389-395.

Meilman, P.W., & Turco, J.H. (1995). On medical withdrawals for mental health reasons. *Journal of American College Health, 40,* 217-227.

Meyer, S., & Schwitzer, A.M. (1999). Stages of identity development among college students with minority sexual orientations. *Journal of College Student Psychotherapy, 13,* 41-65.

Miller, B.E., Miller, M.N., Verhegge, R., Linville, H.H., & Pumariega, A.J. (2002). Alcohol misuse among college athletes: Self-medication for psychiatric symptoms? *Journal of Drug Education, 32,* 41-52.

Mintz, L.B., & Betz, N.E. (1988). Prevalence and correlates of eating disordered behaviors among undergraduate women. *Journal of Counseling Psychology, 35,* 463- 471.

Morgan, E.J., & Cavendish, J.M. (1987). Medical, ethical, and legal issues in treating college student substance abusers. *Alcoholism Treatment Quarterly, 4,* 141-149.

Mori, S. (2000). Addressing the mental health concerns of international students. *Journal of Counseling and Development, 78,* 137-144.

Narikiyo, T.A., & Kameoka, V.A. (1992). Attribution of mental illness and judgments about help seeking among Japanese-American and white American students. *Journal of Counseling Psychology, 39,* 363-369.

Nelson, W.L., Hughes, H.M., Katz, B., & Searight, H.R. (1999). Anorexic eating attitudes and behaviors of male and female college students. *Adolescence, 34,* 621-633.

Nickerson, K.J., Helms, J.E., & Terrell, F. (1994). Cultural mistrust, opinions about mental illness, and black students' attitudes toward seeking psychological help from white counselors. *Journal of Counseling Psychology, 41,* 378-385.

Nishimura, N.J. (1998). Assessing the issues of multiracial students on college campuses. *Journal of College Counseling, 1,* 45-53.

Nolan-Hoeksema, S., & Girgus, J.S. (1994). The emergence of gender differences in depression during adolescence. *Psychological Bulletin, 115,* 424-443.

Norvilitis, J.M., Szablicki, P.B., & Wilson, S.D. (2003). Factors influencing levels of credit-card debt in college students. *Journal of Applied Social Psychology, 33,* 935-947.

O'Malley, K., Wheeler, I., Murphey, J., O'Connell, J., & Waldo, M. (1990). Changes in levels of psychopathology being treated at college and university counseling centers. *Journal of College Student Personnel, 31,* 464-465.

Palma, T.V., & Stanley, J.L. (2002). Effective counseling with lesbian, gay, and bisexual students. *Journal of College Counseling, 5,* 74-89.

Parham, W.D. (1993). The intercollegiate athlete: A 1990's profile. *The Counseling Psychologist, 21,* 411-429.

Pedersen, P.B. (1991). Counseling international students. *The Counseling Psychologist, 19,* 10-58.

Pinkerton, R.S., Hinz, L.D., & Barrow, J.C. (1989). The college student-athlete: Psychological considerations and interventions. *Journal of American College Health, 37,* 218-226.

Pledge, D.S., Lapan, R.T., Heppner, P.P., Kivlighan, D., & Roehlke, H.J. (1998). Stability and severity of presenting problems at a university counseling center: A 6-year analysis. *Professional Psychology: Research and Practice, 29*, 386-389.

Ponterotto, J.G. (1987). Client hospitalization: Issues and considerations for the counselor. *Journal of Counseling and Development, 65*, 542-546.

Prochaska, J.O., DiClemente, C.C., & Norcross, J.C. (1992). In search of how people change: Applications to addictive behaviors. *American Psychologist, 47*, 1102-1114.

Prouty, A.M., Protinsky, H.O., & Canady, D. (2002). College women: Eating behaviors and help-seeking preferences. *Adolescence, 37*, 353-363.

Rawe, J. (2002, June 10). Young and jobless. *Time, 159*, pp. 36-39.

Reifler, C.B., & Liptzin, M.D. (1969). Epidemiological studies of college mental health. *Archives of General Psychiatry, 20*, 528-540.

Rivas-Vazquez, R.A., Johnson, S.L., Rey, G.J., Blais, M.A., & Rivas-Vazquez, A. (2002). Current treatments for bipolar disorder: A review and update for psychologists. *Professional Psychology: Research and Practice, 33*, 212-223.

Rodolfa, E. (1987). Training university faculty to assist emotionally troubled students. *Journal of College Student Personnel, 28*, 183-184.

Rothstein, L.F. (1996). Protections for persons with mental disabilities: Americans with Disabilities Act and related federal and state law. In B.D. Sales & D.W. Shuman (Eds.), *Law, mental health, and mental disorder* (pp. 178-201). Pacific Grove, CA: Brooks/Cole.

Rudd, M.D. (1989). The prevalence of suicidal ideation among college students. *Suicide and Life-Threatening Behavior, 19*, 173-183.

Schulken, E.D., Pinciaro, P.J., Sawyer, R.G., Jensen, J.G., & Hoban, M.T. (1997). Sorority women's body size perceptions and their weight-related attitudes and behaviors. *Journal of American College Health, 46*, 69-74.

Schwartz, A.J., & Whitaker, L.C. (1990). Suicide among college students: Assessment, treatment, and intervention. In S.J. Blumenthal & D.J. Kupfer (Eds.), *Suicide over the life cycle: Risk factors, assessment, and treatment of suicidal patients* (pp. 303-340). Washington, DC: American Psychiatric Press.

Seime, R., & Damer, D. (1991). Identification and treatment of the athlete with an eating disorder. In E.F. Etzel, A.P. Ferrante, & J.W. Pinkney (Eds.), *Counseling college student-athletes: Issues and interventions* (2nd ed., pp. 175-198). Morgantown, WV: Fitness Information Technology, Inc.

Selzer, M.L. (1960). The happy college student myth: Psychiatric implications. *Archives of General Psychiatry, 2*, 131-136.

Sharkin, B.S. (1995). Strains on confidentiality in college-student psychotherapy: Entangled therapeutic relationships, incidental encounters, and third-party inquiries. *Professional Psychology: Research and Practice, 26*, 184-189.

Sharkin, B.S. (1997). Increasing severity of presenting problems in college counseling centers: A closer look. *Journal of Counseling and Development, 75*, 275-281.

Sharkin, B.S. (2004). Assessing changes in categories but not severity of counseling center client problems across 13 years: Comment on Benton, Robertson, Tseng, Newton, and Benton (2003). *Professional Psychology: Research and Practice, 35,* 313-315.

Sharkin, B.S., & Coulter, L.P. (2005). Empirically supporting the increasing severity of college counseling center client problems: Why is it so challenging? *Journal of College Counseling, 8,* 165-171.

Sharkin, B.S., Plageman, P.M., & Mangold, S.L. (2003). College student response to peers in distress: An exploratory study. *Journal of College Student Development, 44,* 691-698.

Sharkin, B.S., Scappaticci, A.G., & Birky, I. (1995). Access to confidential information in a university counseling center: A survey of referral sources. *Journal of College Student Personnel, 36,* 494-495.

Shea, R.H. (2002, February 18). On the edge on campus. *US News & World Report, 132,* pp. 56-57.

Silverman, M.M., Meyer, P.M., Sloane, F., Raffel, M., & Pratt, D.M. (1997). The Big Ten student suicide study: A 10-year study of suicides on midwestern university campuses. *Suicide and Life-Threatening Behavior, 27,* 285-303.

Simon, G.E., Savarino, J., Operskalski, B., & Wang, P.S. (2006). Sucide risk during antidepressant treatment. *American Journal of Psychiatry, 163,* 41-47.

Sontag, D. (2002, April 28). Who was responsible for Elizabeth Shin? *The New York Times Magazine, 151,* 56-61, 94, 139-140.

Steenbarger, B.N. (1998). Alcohol abuse and college counseling: An overview of research and practice. *Journal of College Counseling, 1,* 81-92.

Stein, L. (2004, February 16). A suicide warning. *US News and World Report, 136,* p. 15.

Stone, G.L., & Archer, J. (1990). College and university counseling centers in the 1990s: Challenges and limits. *The Counseling Psychologist, 18,* 539-607.

Stone, G.L., & Lucas, J. (1994). Disciplinary counseling in higher education: A neglected challenge. *Journal of Counseling and Development, 72,* 234-238.

Stone, G.L., Vespia, K.M., & Kanz, J.E. (2000). How good is mental health care on college campuses? *Journal of Counseling Psychology, 47,* 498-510.

Svanum, S., & Zody, Z.B. (2001). Psychopathology and college grades. *Journal of Counseling Psychology, 48,* 72-76.

Tavernise, S. (2003, October 26). In college and in despair; with parents in the dark. *The New York Times,* p. 31.

Twenge, J.M. (2000). The age of anxiety? Birth cohort change in anxiety and neuroticism, 1952-1993. *Journal of Personality and Social Psychology, 79,* 1007-1021.

Uffelman, R.A., & Hardin, S.I. (2002). Session limits at university counseling centers: Effects on help-seeking attitudes. *Journal of Counseling Psychology, 49,* 127-132.

Unger, K. (1998). *Handbook on supported education: Providing services to students with psychiatric disabilities.* Baltimore, MD: Brooks Publishing Co.

VandeCreek, L., Miars, R.D., & Herzog, C.E. (1987). Client anticipations and preferences for confidentiality of records. *Journal of Counseling Psychology, 34,* 62-67.

Voelker, R. (2003). Mounting student depression taxing campus mental health services. *Journal of the American Medical Association, 289,* 2055-2056.

Wahl, O. (1999). *Telling is risky business: Mental health consumers confront stigma.* New Brunswick, NJ: Rutgers University Press.

Walden, C. (1994). The health status of African American college students: A literature review. *Journal of American College Health, 42,* 199-205.

Weber, B., Metha, A., & Nelsen, E. (1997). Relationships among multiple suicide ideation risk factors in college students. *Journal of College Student Psychotherapy, 11,* 49-64.

Wechsler, H., Davenport, A., Dowdall, G., Moeykens, B., & Castillo, S. (1994). Health and behavioral consequences of binge drinking in college: A national survey of students at 140 campuses. *Journal of the American Medical Association, 21,* 1672-1677.

Wechsler, H., Lee, J.E., Kuo, M., & Lee, H. (2000). College binge drinking in the 1990s: A continuing problem: Results of the Harvard School of Public Health 1999 College Alcohol Study. *Journal of American College Health, 48,* 199-210.

Welch, P.J. (1996). In search of a caring community: Group therapy for gay, lesbian and bisexual college students. *Journal of College Student Psychotherapy, 11,* 27-40.

Westefeld, J.S., & Furr, S.R. (1987). Suicide and depression among college students. *Professional Psychology: Research and Practice, 18,* 119-123.

Westefeld, J.S., Maples, M.R., Buford, B., & Taylor, S. (2001) Gay, lesbian, and bisexual college studetns: The relationship between sexual orientation and depression, loneliness, and suicide. *Journal of College Student Psychotherapy, 15,* 71-82.

Whitaker, L.C. (1992). Prescription psychotropic drugs and psychotherapy: Adjunctive or disjunctive? *Journal of College Student Psychotherapy, 7,* 79-92.

White, V.E., Trepal-Wollenzier, H., & Nolan, J.M. (2002). College students and self-injury: Intervention strategies for counselors. *Journal of College Counseling, 5,* 105-113.

Widseth, J.C., Webb, R.E., & John, K.B. (1997). The question of outsourcing: The roles and functions of college counseling services. *Journal of College Student Psychotherapy, 11,* 3-22.

Wiener, E., & Wiener, J. (1997). University students with psychiatric illness: Factors involved in the decision to withdraw from their studies. *Psychiatric Rehabilitation Journal, 20,* 88-91.

Young, J.R. (2003, February 14). Prozac campus: More students seek counseling and take psychiatric medication. *The Chronicle of Higher Education, 49,* pp. A37-A38.

Index

College Students in Distress
© 2006 by The Haworth Press, Inc. All rights reserved.
doi:10.1300/5228_10

Order a copy of this book with this form or online at:
http://www.haworthpress.com/store/product.asp?sku=5228

COLLEGE STUDENTS IN DISTRESS
A Resource Guide for Faculty, Staff, and Campus Community

_____in hardbound at $34.95 (ISBN-13: 978-0-7890-2524-1; ISBN-10: 0-7890-2524-8)

_____in softbound at $19.95 (ISBN-13: 978-0-7890-2525-8; ISBN-10: 0-7890-2525-6)

Or order online and use special offer code HEC25 in the shopping cart.

COST OF BOOKS_____

POSTAGE & HANDLING_____
*(US: $4.00 for first book & $1.50
for each additional book)*
*(Outside US: $5.00 for first book
& $2.00 for each additional book)*

SUBTOTAL_____

IN CANADA: ADD 7% GST_____

STATE TAX_____
*(NJ, NY, OH, MN, CA, IL, IN, PA, & SD
residents, add appropriate local sales tax)*

FINAL TOTAL_____
*(If paying in Canadian funds,
convert using the current
exchange rate, UNESCO
coupons welcome)*

☐ **BILL ME LATER:** (Bill-me option is good on
US/Canada/Mexico orders only; not good to
jobbers, wholesalers, or subscription agencies.)
☐ Check here if billing address is different from
shipping address and attach purchase order and
billing address information.

Signature_____

☐ **PAYMENT ENCLOSED: $_____**

☐ **PLEASE CHARGE TO MY CREDIT CARD.**

☐ Visa ☐ MasterCard ☐ AmEx ☐ Discover
☐ Diner's Club ☐ Eurocard ☐ JCB

Account # _____

Exp. Date_____

Signature_____

Prices in US dollars and subject to change without notice.

NAME_____

INSTITUTION_____

ADDRESS_____

CITY_____

STATE/ZIP_____

COUNTRY_____ COUNTY (NY residents only)_____

TEL_____ FAX_____

E-MAIL_____

May we use your e-mail address for confirmations and other types of information? ☐ Yes ☐ No
We appreciate receiving your e-mail address and fax number. Haworth would like to e-mail or fax special
discount offers to you, as a preferred customer. **We will never share, rent, or exchange your e-mail address
or fax number.** We regard such actions as an invasion of your privacy.

Order From Your Local Bookstore or Directly From
The Haworth Press, Inc.
10 Alice Street, Binghamton, New York 13904-1580 • USA
TELEPHONE: 1-800-HAWORTH (1-800-429-6784) / Outside US/Canada: (607) 722-5857
FAX: 1-800-895-0582 / Outside US/Canada: (607) 771-0012
E-mail to: orders@haworthpress.com

For orders outside US and Canada, you may wish to order through your local
sales representative, distributor, or bookseller.
For information, see http://haworthpress.com/distributors

(Discounts are available for individual orders in US and Canada only, not booksellers/distributors.)

PLEASE PHOTOCOPY THIS FORM FOR YOUR PERSONAL USE.
http://www.HaworthPress.com   BOF06